How To Do Spiritual Warfare

Workbook

MICHAEL VAN VLYMEN

ISBN 10-1500873780
ISBN 13-978-1500873783

This book is available from www.amazon.com and may be ordered through booksellers and book distributors worldwide.

INTRODUCTION

There are a ton of books available on the topic of spiritual warfare., so why did I feel compelled to write this workbook? The truth is I "fought" the Lord on this much more than I would like to admit. *"Lord"* I said, *"There are a great many books on this subject by people much brighter than I. Plus, everyone already knows this stuff anyway."* I argued.

Then one week as the Lord and I were discussing this, I was driving home from work and listening to a favorite Christian radio show, when they announced that the guest that day would be talking about his new book on spiritual warfare. Awesome! I thought. *"See Lord? It's covered."* I enjoyed listening to the show. I could tell he knew something about the subject and although he didn't say it, I kind of thought that he had probably cast out evil spirits before. (Always a good sign if you are talking about this subject) He quoted all the right scriptures and talked about how powerful the name and the blood were. However, during the call in segment of the show was when it all began to fall apart in my opinion. A woman called to ask about a specific problem. One of her children was experiencing ongoing demonic attacks at night and it had been going on for so long, she was at the end of her rope. And I'm very sorry to say that although the man quoted the right scriptures and tried to encourage her, he gave her no practical advice whatsoever. None. It was sobering. The Lord was making His point.

"But Lord" I said, *"That is just some guy like me that I have never even heard of. I know there are people who do know about these things."* Almost as if in answer to my argument , the very next week, same channel different program, there was a very famous preacher that was giving a several part series on spiritual warfare. I won't say his name, but if I did you would recognize it. I thought *"I'm really going to enjoy this."* I thought it was great that such an important topic was getting some attention.

The man was eloquent. He had a beautiful speaking voice and delivery. He spoke and painted such beautiful pictures with his words, he could have brought me to tears. He spoke of Roman armies during the time of Christ, gleaming swords, the whole armor of God, laying out each point flawlessly and magnificently. He gave wonderful analogies and talked about how powerful our God is to overcome the enemy in our lives. I know that you know where this is going. After the second installment of the series, I realized that he was not going to come even close to presenting anything that would be helpful to those who really needed this kind of help.

"Ok Lord, I give"

This book was written to give you very specific answers and explanations to allow you to immediately begin to take back what enemy has taken from you. There will be foundational things all based in scripture that I believe are imperative and we will then move to other issues surrounding warfare and deliverance and how to address specific areas of life, such as personal holiness and walking a victorious life, doing warfare on behalf of your family and/or unsaved loved ones, and keeping the evil one out of your home, life and circumstances.

This workbook will not be all encompassing by any means. There are several good books that can give you a more in depth understanding as you begin to engage in this warfare. But it is set up to be used as a guide to help you engage more effectively in spiritual warfare. It may be used in a group setting, but may also be used by a single person who would like to have a little more structure in pursuing a greater knowledge and effectiveness in spiritual warfare.

Having once been where many of you are right now, I did not want you to have to go through an in depth treatise on warfare and then *still* have to decide *"Where do I start?"*

As someone who sees at times into the spirit realm, into the world of angels and demons I will talk about many things as if I have actually seen how it works, because I have.

Michael

PREPARATIONS FOR GROUP STUDY

If you are using this guide in a group setting there are a few things you can do to make the atmosphere more conducive to learning.

1st Invest in stick on name tags and a couple of markers. In group settings it's rare if everyone knows everyone else. With the name tags, those who don't know the others will feel more comfortable to engage in conversation if they are not struggling over names.

2nd Get some blank business cards or note cards and extra pens enough for the group. It will give people the option of getting connected with others to support each other in prayer or warfare. Also pick up some inexpensive spiral notebooks for those who don't have, or can't afford workbooks. Not everyone knows what to bring.

3rd Consider providing coffee or tea or water and possibly a light snack of some sort. Although this isn't really "social hour" it should be a relaxed and comfortable learning environment. Warfare should be so natural to us that we can discuss it in a coffee shop or someone's living room. We don't want to present this as spooky or religious in any way.

4th Ask the group to place their cell phones on vibrate during the classes. This will keep the distractions to a minimum. There's not much worse than trying to bare your soul about some terrific need in your life or family only to be interrupted by a funny ringtone and someone getting up to take the call. It conveys the wrong message sometimes and can definitely interrupt the flow.

5th Encourage everyone to feel comfortable to ask questions and be engaged. In many group study situations there are people who feel very comfortable sharing and some who don't. Draw people into the discussions so everyone can be involved. (I have been to such groups where the same 4 or 5 people do all the talking while everyone else just listens. You don't want that.)

6th Take a few minutes to greet everyone and appreciate those who came.

CONTENTS

ACKNOWLEDGMENTS

I would like to acknowledge and thank all those who have taught me about the things pertinent to this subject. My dad Marvin Van Vlymen, Derek Prince and Frank Hammond. Also I would like to thank those who I have learned from more recently about warfare, authority and the normalcy of moving in the supernatural of God. That would include Neville Johnson, Dr. Bruce Allen, Mel Bond, Don Basham and Ana Mendez Ferrell.

1

REALITY OF SPIRITUAL WARFARE

Be sober, be vigilant; because your adversary the devil, as a roaring lion, walketh about, seeking whom he may devour: (1 Peter 5:8)

Put on the whole armour of God, that ye may be able to stand against the wiles of the devil. (Ephesians 6:11)

For we wrestle not against flesh and blood, but against principalities, against powers, against the rulers of the darkness of this world, against spiritual wickedness in high places. (Ephesians 6:12)

Submit yourselves therefore to God. Resist the devil, and he will flee from you. (James 4:7)

The previous four verses make it very clear that we have a real enemy and a real battle. There are many, many more scriptures that address this subject. All throughout the bible you can find references to spiritual warfare and the fact that we have an enemy whose desire is to steal, kill and destroy. (John 10:10)

The fact is that this has not changed from biblical times until now. If people living back then in societies where women stayed covered up, there were no ungodly movies, music or TV shows and they still had to deal with people being afflicted by evil spirits, how much more us today? The fact is that evil spirits *openly* manifest their presence nowadays and most of the world considers it normal behavior.

Lots of Battlegrounds

What are some of the areas that they had to deal with? Many of the same things that we deal with also.

In Mark chapter nine we see the disciples trying to cast an evil spirit from a young boy but couldn't do it. Jesus told them to bring the boy to Him and then He cast it out. The spirit was causing epileptic type seizures that were making the boy throw himself into the water or into the fire.

In Luke thirteen, Jesus heals a woman who is crippled by loosing her from a spirit of infirmity. He also called her a daughter of Abraham so this wasn't some "heathen" person but a covenant child of God.

And of course the demoniac of the Gadarenes in Mark chapter five Jesus confronted the evil spirits in the man whose behavior was that of a lunatic. Jesus commanded the spirits to leave and the man immediately was in his right mind and got dressed and thanked the Lord for his deliverance.

There are many more examples in scripture, covering a great many areas but the point is that we can look *at our own lives* or the lives of family or loved ones and see that there are issues where we have to have supernatural help from above.

How many family members are battling sicknesses? How many illnesses do we see among the believers we know? How many family members that want nothing to do with "your religion" (God) ? How many kids suddenly turn rebellious for seemingly no reason? How many jobs lost or raises missed or promotions given to someone else when you are the one who earned it? How many marriages barely hanging on and you can't even make yourself believe that God could fix it? Depression, anger, unrealized dreams, mistreatment, accidents, bad dreams, weird happenings around your home or your life and the list goes on and on because any and every area that the enemy can take he will take.

Don't be Discouraged!

It looks like a laundry list of heartache but the great news is that every area is redeemable! If you don't see your particular issues listed, that's ok, The authority given us by the Lord Jesus Christ has it covered. This is not some impossible battle either! You don't have to be a "super saint" and you don't have to worry that somehow you won't measure up to the task. The authority and power of Jesus Christ is absolute. And you, as a believer have legal rights to use His authority. Period.

Wild Dogs

Before we go any further I would like to give you a simple analogy to show you how normal this topic *should* be.

Let's say that somehow, a couple of wild dogs were able to sneak into your house. You don't know how they got in, someone left a door open or wasn't paying attention or whatever, but the fact is that they are there. They are sneaky and are causing a mess and making your home unlivable. What would a normal reaction be? When you find out what the problem is, you take a big stick, maybe even get a friend involved if you have to **and chase them out!**

You don't worry about what people will say! *"What will sister so and so say if she ever found out that wild dogs snuck into our home?" "Maybe people will think less of us or think we are bad people that we have this problem."* No, the only real shame would be in allowing those wild dogs to mess up your life because of some weird sense of pride or rejection. This is a real issue because I know people who deal with this. (The fear, not the dogs)

Don't live your life in pain so that people who don't love you anyway will think better of you. Life is too short for that and there is no up-side.

What are your areas that need to see the power of God manifested? Make a list with the most important things first if you can. If you have sensitive areas and are afraid someone might somehow see this list, make it in some kind of "code" that only you know what it means. Make the list cover every possible thing that the Holy Spirit brings to mind.

1. _____

2. _____

3. _____

4. _____

5. _____

6. _____

7. _____

8. _____

9. _____

10. _____

11. _____

12. _____

13. _____

14. _____

15. _____

16. _____

17. _____

18. _____

19. _____

20. _____

The Stigma of Evil Spirits and Christians

One of the things I tried to do with my wild dog story was to show that we should not get caught up in any crazy posturing about being afflicted by the enemy. There is a stigma among a great many Christian groups and denominations about the reality of evil spirits, why they are there, how they got there, what did the person do etc..

Many Christians, because of what they have been taught will not even allow themselves to be prayed for because they believe that evil spirits can't bother Christians. Many others try to rationalize or justify this by talking about whether it's obsession or oppression or depression, certainly not possession! (I prefer the simple "afflicted")

In the Bible , did the woman who was crippled argue about what Jesus was saying about her? *"Are you implying I'm possessed Jesus!?"*

If you are going to be effective as a spiritual warrior for yourself, your family or for anybody else, you have to get past all of that. Simplify. Wild dogs....Let's chase them out.

Make it Normal

There is nothing in the world like freedom so we have to make this normal so that people will receive it. **Yes, evil spirits can and do afflict Christians. The Bible is also clear on this.**

Know ye not, that to whom ye yield yourselves servants to obey, his servants ye are to whom ye obey; whether of sin unto death, or of obedience unto righteousness? (Romans 6:16)

Do you remember when Jesus rebuked Peter?

But when he had turned about and looked on his disciples, he rebuked Peter, saying, Get thee behind me, Satan: for thou savourest not the things that be of God, but the things that be of men. (Mark 8:33)

Do you think Jesus said it that way because it was true, or because he was really angry with Peter and wanted to take him down a notch? An insult to put him in his place.

No, we have to take away the stigma of driving evil spirits out of the lives of Christians. I am emphasizing this because I know there are people who reject deliverance because they don't think they can be afflicted.

I heard a story of a pastor who suffered for five years with debilitating headaches. No amount of prayer had helped and medicine had not helped either. One day a friend of his who had only recently began learning about spiritual warfare and deliverance suggested to his friend. "Perhaps it's an evil spirit. Do you mind if I try to cast it out?" The pastor who had been suffering said "By all means give it a shot." So the friend began rebuking this evil spirit who was causing this pain in his friend. After a few minutes an evil spirit actually spoke through the pastor and said his name was pain and that he had been there many years. When the friend said "What are you doing there?! He is a believer and a pastor!" The evil spirit responded "No one ever told me I had to go." The spirit then was cast out and the man healed of his pain.

Does that stretch you? How about this then. The famous Bible teacher / minister Derek Prince had been having severe stomach pain for years. One day a lowly worker in one of the churches he visited came to him and said *"do you mind if I pray for you?"* Brother Derek, just to be polite allowed the man to pray but really didn't expect anything from it. Well... the man rebuked an evil spirit and commanded it to leave and Derek was healed and delivered that day!

This is not a spooky subject. It is normal supernatural Christian life. The supernatural, spiritual realms must become normal to us. We will discuss that more later, but for now,

What are some ways that we can make this (supernatural) normal?

1. _____
2. _____
3. _____
4. _____
5. _____
6. _____
7. _____
8. _____

Everyday , Everywhere...

I mentioned that the reality is that evil spirits openly manifest their presence nowadays without much concern that they will be challenged. If you walk close to God, you probably experience this a lot. If you carry a strong anointing upon your life or spend a lot of time in God's presence or glory, it will be even more so.

You may not immediately see this but let me point out a few things that may convince you. Have you ever been in a checkout line at the store, watched the cashier smile and be pleasant with others but when your turn comes they are suddenly cold and rude? Have you ever had people walk past you and when they get very close to you they suddenly belch loudly or break wind? Have you ever come across people who suddenly start muttering angrily when they get close to you? Ever been to a party where everyone in the room is nasty to you for no obvious reason? I have actually had people literally growl at me in public places.

These are the things that we experience every day, and when you start to pay attention it gets real obvious. Once I was walking into a store and some angry looking man was walking out mumbling something. I listened carefully and what he was saying was " You Christians really think you're something don't you?" There was no one else around for the man to be talking to. A spirit was making his presence known.

Sometimes people will get very agitated with you because their demons are agitated with you. The people don't even know why they feel that way. Most of us do not have to think very hard to recall these types of seemingly random incidents in our lives.

Weird Goings On

If you are in a group setting, jog your memories and talk about a few of these things. Has everyone experienced this? Is there a common denominator? Was the encounter preceded by prayer or worship or anything else that may have "triggered" it?

1. _____

2. _____

3. _____

4. _____

5. _____

Where is the Disconnect?

Ok. If the warfare is real and we are the body of Christ, why are so many afflicted and seemingly in defeat? If the Bible is true and we are more than conquerors through Christ why are we experiencing the same kind of problems, sickness and bondages as the people outside the church? All those great bible verses and yet still little or no victory. What is the problem? We are serious. We love Jesus. What does it take for the manifestation of God's promises over our lives?

The Religious Church

A part of the problem is that our relationship with God has become religious. No I don't mean that we are insincere, but rather that we have "done" church the same way for so many decades that it is like a comfortable old shoe. We live our lives, try to be good, pray for our friends and families and come together on Sundays to worship and listen to a (hopefully) great sermon. We sit in the same pew, usually talk to the same friends, enjoy our fellowship, enjoy the worship and then go home and do it all again next week. It is a nice, religious routine even if God does move sometimes.

I'm not trying to shift blame onto your church or your pastor either. People have come to expect these things. I will be honest and say that I have looked at my watch around noon just like a lot of people.

If the Holy Spirit is not directing things, whether it is your church or your life, the flow and power of the Spirit will be absent. Non supernatural church means no supernatural power to effect change. We might enjoy the service but the serious stuff will remain untouched. I'm not just talking about mainline churches but spirit filled churches as well.

Most church services in nearly every church I have ever been to fit into this mold. Lately, things have begun to change but it is still a work in progress.

It usually looks something like this....

You arrive at church. You greet friends for a few minutes. Get your water bottle or coffee (in the newer charismatic churches) Spend about 45 minutes to an hour in worship, announcements and such. Then a prayer, a sermon and at the end an announcement..."God bless you. You are dismissed. If anyone here needs prayer, prayer team members will be available. Ten am until noon. I know not every church looks exactly like this but my point is that most of us have a routine. It's not just being orderly, it's a routine. (I do realize there has to be order. I'm not speaking of that.)

What can we do to break out of that cycle or mindset? Pray and ask the Holy Spirit *"What are your desires today?"* Maybe instead of walking in and greeting friends the Lord will instruct you to do a three lap prayer walk around the church before things start. Maybe the Lord will tell you to go up front during worship and lift your hands. Maybe He will tell you to encourage someone. We should never have to turn on the supernatural. That is where we are supposed to be living.

What does your own routine look like?

1._____

2._____

3._____

4._____

5._____

6._____

7._____

8._____

What could you do differently? How could you flow with the Spirit more and bring a greater anointing to your own group?

1._____

2._____

3._____

4._____

5._____

6._____

7._____

8._____

Please don't get the impression that I'm trying to say that you are not following the Holy Spirit. I'm just trying to get you to "shake yourself."

What does all this stuff have to do with spiritual warfare anyway? The power, the anointing, the presence of God we are talking about walking in or manifesting is not an event, but rather a lifestyle. This all plays a part.

Our Discomfort

Another part of the problem is that we are uncomfortable with the supernatural, particularly when it comes to the demonic. This discomfort goes across the board from the staunch religious person to the spirit filled believer operating in the spiritual gifts. Here is what I mean....

On one end of the spectrum you have the person who believes the Bible is a nice collection of religious stories and they go to church and read the book because it is their "religious tradition." Then you have the person who believes in the truth of the Gospel and is born again with a real relationship with God, but they don't believe there is any more to it than that. Then you have the person who is saved and believes in healing, so long as they don't know how or why it happened and it isn't too weird. Then you have the person who believes in healing and that they can be a part of it by laying hands on the sick according to the scripture.

This description goes through a long list of gradual changes until you get to the person on the other end that believes that everything God has ever done, He still does, and everything He has ever done for any person in the Bible He will do for you, and you can even do greater works than Jesus, because He said you would.

So most Christians have a line that they won't cross over. I will believe this far and no more. Spiritual warfare is one of those lines. *"I will believe for the beautiful happy stuff but not this stuff."*

If you think this observation is not correct, let me ask you how many Christians do you think have ever said these words. *"Come out in Jesus' name!"*

I am believing that you either do or will go as far as you have to go to experience the full weight and measure of the power of the blood covenant of Jesus Christ in your life.

What are your own lines? (I will believe this but not this)

1. _____

2. _____

3. _____

4. _____

5. _____

And because we generally try to come into "agreement" with whatever group we are a part of, what are the lines your group or your family won't go past?

1. _____

2. _____

3. _____

4. _____

5. _____

Now the important part...

Are you willing to say *"Holy Spirit I will go as far as you want me to go. No reservations, and no limits."* If you are willing to give the Lord that much it will put all of the responsibility on Him, where it belongs.

Take a few minutes and really pray that the Lord Himself will direct your path in this regard. That only His will and His truth will be your reality. Tell Him you want no deceptions of the enemy, only His light and truth and that you will receive it. That position of your heart is a safety measure that you can count on! If we ask for bread He won't give us a stone! (Matthew 7:9-11)

If you are part of a group, take advantage of the prayer of agreement and pray over each person that god's truth will be manifest on this subject and His power. That the spirit of Wisdom and Revelation would come upon each one.

Another reason that God's people are so defeated nowadays is because they don't really know who they really are....

2

WHO YOU REALLY ARE

Beloved, now are we the sons of God, and it doth not yet appear what we shall be: but we know that, when he shall appear, we shall be like him; for we shall see him as he is.
(1 John 3:2)

Study to shew thyself approved unto God, a workman that needeth not to be ashamed, rightly dividing the word of truth. (2 Timothy 2:15)

Ok, It's not that most people don't know who they are. Many of us know or at least have read or heard all the verses about who we are in Christ. It's just that the promises and covenants and statements about who we are seem way too over the top for most people to actually believe them in a literal way. Going straight to one of the big ones, how many people *actually* believe that they can or will do greater works than Jesus Christ himself did according to John 14:12 ?

Verily, verily, I say unto you, He that believeth on me, the works that I do shall he do also; and greater works than these shall he do; because I go unto my Father.
(John 14:12)

Doubt and Unbelief

Based on the belief that no one will ever do greater things than Jesus did, (even though *He* said they would) the majority of the Bible believing church has come to believe that this scripture is saying that greater means greater amounts of salvation or greater work of the Holy Spirit for salvation. It only stands to reason that because the majority of the church world believes the only "supernatural " manifestation of God available to believers today is salvation, then the only "greater work" would be salvation also.

It sounds very humble and "holy" to believe that. *"No brother, I'm just an old sinner saved by grace. I could never do the things that Jesus did."* But in reality it is veiled disobedience. In the scriptures the Lord gave clear instructions to us as to what He expects His followers to do.   One such example is Matthew 10:8. It doesn't get much clearer than this.

Heal the sick, cleanse the lepers, raise the dead, cast out devils: freely ye have received, freely give. (Matthew 10:8)

The same reason people give for not doing the things Jesus told us to do are the things Jesus told us to do! *"Only the Lord can do something like that."*

Veiled disobedience. Here is a short explanation why. Let's say that you are going out of town for a month and you have entrusted to your son (or daughter) the job of maintaining the yard while you are gone. *" Here is all the equipment you'll need, mower, weed whacker, hedge trimmers, and I've also written out easy to follow directions of what to do and how to do it, so just follow the simple steps and you will be fine."* Now a month later you arrive home and find the yard totally grown over and unkempt. Being a merciful parent, you realize there must be a good legitimate reason that your child did not do the simple task given. When you ask why, here is what you are told. *" Who am **I** to believe that **I** could ever do what only **you** can do. Who am **I** to believe that **I** could cut the grass like you. Only **you** can keep the yard nice. To believe otherwise would be pride on my part ."* (looking sincere and humble)

Would you feel special that they thought so highly of you or would you be angry that they did not obey such a simple thing in light of all you do for them?

I make this example because I hear this so much from fellow Christians who have been taught that Jesus couldn't really have meant all that "over the top" stuff, so there has to be another explanation. If you want to walk in the power that lets you drive out devils and be successful in spiritual warfare, you must realize, or at the very least allow the Holy Spirit to make you aware, that you are *literally* everything Jesus said you are.

Who You Are in Christ

I have given you authority to trample on snakes and scorpions and to overcome all the power of the enemy; nothing will harm you. (Luke 10:19)

Once you realize, or begin to realize who you are, you will begin to use the authority given you, and in greater measure. This authority or position in Christ crosses all boundaries into every area of your life. Whether at home or work, in your relationships, family and friends, you can exercise or exert the authority given you to effect all areas.

This includes authority over sicknesses and illness, addictions, bad habits, mental illness, your finances, salvation of family and friends. You name it and you can influence it or change it, period.

We are not talking about exerting control over someone's free will, that would constitute witchcraft. Yes even Christians can unknowingly work in a spirit of witchcraft by praying their personal will for someone to come to pass.

God's will for someone is what we are to pray. Thy will be done. If you know God's will on a particular matter, you can pray it. " Lord please heal Jonathan." Or " I rebuke sickness is his life and command it to leave in Jesus' name." God has clearly made His will to be known concerning healing so you can pray it with great confidence. We know from scripture that Jesus healed all. That is His will. There are no examples in the Word of Him telling anyone "It's not the Father's will to heal you." or " God put this on you to make you a better person." No, we know God's will concerning this matter.

The same goes for salvation. We have assurance that The Lord desires for all to be saved as well, so we can pray with bold confidence about this also.

The Lord is not slow in keeping His promise, as some understand slowness. Instead He is patient with you, not wanting anyone to perish, but everyone to come to repentance. (2 Peter 3:9)

God is not wishy washy. He has established who He is to us so we are not confused about how to pray. We are to exercise the authority given to us. No more of those prayers "Lord we don't know what you want to do about so and so's sickness or bondage or salvation, but if it be your will... If we honestly don't know God's will, we must get in the word until we know Him a little better. God's will and His mandate toward us is very clear concerning how we are to address the enemy. This gives us full assurance as we engage in spiritual warfare. It is difficult to pray with much conviction if we think that it may be God who is afflicting us or is desiring our affliction for some reason.

Our Identity is Key

When we accept Christ as Savior and Lord, we become a different person or a different being. A new creation. Something supernatural happens and yes we literally becomes a new creation. In addition, we inherit a position in Christ of authority in the realm of the Kingdom of God. You are no longer human beings as such but something far, far greater.

... Are you not acting like mere humans? (1 Corinthians 3:3)

Therefore if any man be in Christ, he is a new creature...

(2 Corinthians 5:17)

It is so very important to take hold of everything in the Word of God that gives you legal position in the spiritual realms. (as well as this natural realm)

What are some Bible verses that tell us who we are in Christ? What does the verse mean in a real and useful way? How can we apply the verse in real life?

1. _____

2. _____

3. _____

4. _____

5. _____

6. _____

7. _____

8. _____

9. _____

10. _____

11. _____

12. _____

Here are a few that I like...

You are a son (daughter) of God

Beloved, now are we the sons of God, and it doth not yet appear what we shall be: but we know that when He shall appear, we shall be like Him; for we shall see Him as He is. (1 John 3:2)

You are a member of God's own household.

Consequently, you are no longer foreigners and strangers, but fellow citizens with God's people and also members of His household. (Ephesians 2:19)

You are heirs of God

And if children, then heirs; heirs of God and joint heirs with Christ; if so be that we suffer with Him, so that we may be also glorified together. (Romans 8:17)

You are loved of God and chosen by Him

For we know, brothers and sisters loved by God, that He has chosen you. (1 Thessalonians 1:4)

You are a citizen of Heaven

But we are citizens of Heaven, where the Lord Jesus Christ lives. And we are eagerly waiting for Him to return as our Savior. (Philippians 3:20)

These are just a few of the many scriptures that talk about who you are. When the Word talks about you being a son, or an heir or a member of God's family, because God is making these statements it is as a legal, binding document. We have, on the authority of God's own word, legal rights established by God Himself. This is our true identity and this is the reality and identity that should be manifest in our lives. This is a foundational key for exercising authority over the enemy.

But like many things God has given us, there is a choice involved. We have free will to lay hold of this or not. The promises are taken hold of by faith and made manifest. It's a choice. There is a scripture that says that we are to submit ourselves to God and resist the devil, and he will flee. It is our *choice* however whether we do this. We can resist the devil 'til we are blue in the face and not see him move off of our lives if we don't *choose* to do the first part also. For many however, we are submitting to God, we just don't know how to actively "resist the devil." We will present that after we establish a few things about who we are and the authority we have been given.

You are a co-worker of God   (2 Corinthians 6:1)
You are a saint   (Ephesians 1:18)
You are a dwelling for Holy Spirit (Ephesians 2:22)
You are protected   (John 10:28)
You are more than a conqueror   (Romans 8:37)
You are the righteousness of God (2 Corinthians 5:21)
You are a king and priest   (Revelations 1:6)

There are many more that you can dig out in your Bible study time, but these are some of my personal favorites concerning who we are.

Our Authority is Key

Next, we need to consider what our authorities are, what our promises are and what our positions in Christ are. These are also vital things not just to be aware of but to really, really know them. Here are some of my favorite scriptures that I take hold of every day. I'm going somewhere with all this so please hang in there.

God's Provisions for Warfare

You are seated in Heavenly places

And God raised us up with Christ and seated us with Him in the heavenly realms in Christ Jesus. (Ephesians 2:6)

You have been given authority

Behold, I have given you authority to tread on serpents and scorpions, and over all the power of the enemy, and nothing shall hurt you. (Luke 10:19)

Powerful signs will follow you

And these signs will accompany those who believe: in my name they will cast out demons; they will speak in new tongues; they will pick up serpents with their hands; and if they drink any deadly poison, it will not hurt them; they will lay hands on the sick, and they will recover.
(Mark 16:17,18)

You have been given a mandate

Heal the sick, cleanse the lepers, raise the dead, cast out devils: freely ye have received, freely give. (Matthew 10:8)

He has given His angels charge over you

If you say, "The Lord is my refuge," and you make the Most High your dwelling, no harm will overtake you, no disaster will come near your tent. For He will command His angels concerning you, to guard you in all your ways; They will lift you up in their hands, so that you will not strike your foot against a stone. (Psalm 91: 9 – 12)

If you resist the devil, he will flee.

Therefore submit to God. Resist the devil and he will flee from you. (James 4:7)

You have a right to use the powerful name of Jesus

Therefore God has highly exalted Him and given Him the name which is above every name, that at the name of Jesus every knee shall bow, of those in Heaven, and of those on Earth, and of those under the Earth. (Philippians 2:9,10)

The greater one is in you

Little children, you are from God and have overcome them, for He who is in you is greater than he who is in the world.

(1 John 4:4)

The Authority of the Believer

Make a list of the scriptures on the authority of the believer that you like, or that "speak" to you. The verse does not have directly pertain to spiritual warfare. For example the scripture

"I can do all things through Christ[a] who strengthens me." (Philippians 4:13)

Many people use Philippians 4:19 as a reminder or an encouragement for physical strength to get through the day or if they are facing some challenge in everyday life, but a verse like this is an open invitation to use across the board in every area of your life. Don't limit yourself as you build your collection of authority verses.

1. _____

2. _____

31

3. _____

4. _____

5. _____

6. _____

7. _____

8. _____

9. _____

10. _____

"Knowing" the scripture is not enough

There is a reason that I asked you to choose the scriptures that speak to you personally. It's easier to live in your own revelation as opposed to someone else's.

The Bible says that even the demons believe and tremble. It's not enough to know and it's not enough to believe. Everything must become a reality in your life. Your reality. When God's reality begins to manifest in and around your life, it doesn't matter what anyone says or believes about it. It will be reality. I have many people around my life that don't really believe in angels and the manifest presence of God today, but when they are in our home they have seen them or felt God's presence. That is the manifest reality in our lives and if an unbeliever comes into our environment, it doesn't negate that that reality. People have told us they have seen "ghosts" or "beings" walking around in our home. Because they don't accept the reality of angels, they still have to call them something so they choose the explanation and terminology the world uses.

How do the promises of God begin to become manifest in your life? Is there something we can do other than pray and read the Bible?

Putting it all Together
Decree!

Having an understanding of who you are and what your authority is, gives you the basis for putting together a great decree to speak over your own life. I like to decree or declare who I am in Christ every day to put the spirit realm on notice that I know who I am and I know what belongs to me. I also like to do this to remind myself of who I am. I know that may sound strange but many times the enemy will try to get our minds thinking about solving problems with our natural understanding, so that we don't move in the supernatural power of God. As children of God, supernatural should be our first option.

Go through your list and possibly even get some more verses and choose the verses that mean the most to you, then put them together in a declaration you can speak over yourself every day. As a warrior of the Kingdom, you will find this to be important and significant for you. This position that you are claiming is the basis for your legal right to destroy the works of the enemy.

My personal decree

In Jesus' name, I am a son of God. I am seated at God's own right hand in Jesus Christ. I am loved of my Father in Heaven. He loves me with an eternal love and I am a member of God's own household. I am an heir of God and a joint heir with Jesus Christ. I am a legal heir of my Father's kingdom. I am seated in authority in heavenly places in Christ far above principalities and powers. He has given His angels charge over me. I am clean and holy and clothed in His righteousness. The devil has no place in me and no power over me. And even on my worst day, I am still a son of God and my feelings have nothing to do with that.

I normally make this declaration or decree as I get ready for work. Sometimes I add in other verses or statements concerning who I am in Christ depending on what I am dealing with. Sometimes I will repeat it several times because although my emotions don't have to be "on board" for it to be true, I like to be in agreement in spirit, soul and body.

The last statement in my decree I added because of a teaching I heard from Neville Johnson. Brother Neville gave an analogy when teaching about spiritual authority comparing believers to police officers. He said that when an officer has a bad day or doesn't feel good or gets in an argument with their spouse they don't stop being a police officer. They still have the authority of their position whether they "feel" like it or not. He says it's the same with us. Our feelings have nothing to do with the fact that we as believers are seated in authority in Christ. We still have the authority of Christ even on our worst days. That's a very good thing to know.

This segment about our identity and authority is meant to lay out a plan or foundation from which you can do warfare. That's why I'm asking you to do this. I have found this to be effective for many reasons and I know it will be for you also.

Your Decree

As you put together your own decree of who you are in Christ, choose the scriptures that Holy Spirit leads you to. Write out all the scriptures in a way so that it flows naturally off of your tongue or you have a real good feeling about it.

This decree should be just as natural and as easy to speak as if you were telling someone your name , address and phone number. Know it that well and better.

Something very important to remember about this decree is that this is not you trying to encourage yourself or psych yourself up. Because of who you are, the words you speak have incredible power. When you decree things, things happen in the spiritual realm, which is the entire point of doing this. (Think Mark 11:23) As you make decrees the things afflicting you or preventing you are either destroyed or moved off of you. Doubt and unbelief become displaced. Fear is driven out.

As you first begin to speak your decree over yourself and your own life, do it until you notice a shift take place. At first it may feel like you are just giving yourself a pep-talk, but do it until your spirit manifests the reality of it. Like anything worthwhile in the Kingdom, you may have to lay hold of it by force., especially on this topic.

I have been doing this for quite a while and I still have to "break through" barriers sometimes when I do this . You can experience this also with prayer or praise. I have spoken to many people who tell me that the first twenty minutes they pray or worship, it "feels" like they are faking it. That is just the process of breaking through. The soulish things that try to stifle your spirit man as you contend for the promises and provision of God.

MY DECREE

_____

_____

_____

_____

_____

_____

_____

_____

_____

_____

I know that to people who question the whole idea that God is still very present in our lives, this will indeed seem like some kind of exercise in talking yourself into something. Like *"Maybe if I say it enough times I will begin to believe it."*

But the reality of the decree I base on Job 22:28

"You will also decree a thing, and it will be established for you; And light will shine on your ways." (Job 22:28)

Also Proverbs 23:7

"For as he thinks in his heart, so is he." (Proverbs 23:7)

One very important thing that I learned as I began to try to lay hold of manifested spiritual realities is this...

"What you focus on , you connect with and when you connect, activation takes place."

In the anointed and groundbreaking book "Gazing into Glory" by Dr. Bruce Allen you can learn about this reality *and how to access it for your own life* in much more detail and I would encourage you to do that. Just this one key alone can take you to places in God that can change everything for you. For now however, I want to show you the reality of what I am talking about.

Take the decree you have created with you and situate yourself quietly to spend a few minutes focusing on the Lord. (like in prayer or waiting on God) Sitting very still, no moving about, begin to state your decree. If you have to open your eyes to look at what you have written, that's ok. Look at your decree and then close your eyes and begin to speak this truth over yourself. Say it quietly but aloud a few times and then say it in your mind / imagination If you quiet yourself and do this, because you are yielding to the spirit man (i.e. Sitting still and not moving about) you will feel your spirit stir. When the spiritual begins to manifest and you can feel it, it brings a greater understanding that this is a reality.

Although I state my decree when I am up and moving around in the mornings, I also do this at night when no one is up and around to distract me. Between the quiet and the dark and the absence of movement, there is nothing for my natural man, my physical being to get distracted by. When I state my decree in this situation , The presence of God, the angelic presence, the obvious feeling of your spirit is exponentially multiplied. You lay hold of this experience and try to take it with you into your everyday life. (That subject deserves more time and explanation and is for another book)

During my own times of waiting on God in the night watch as they call it, I have had everything from electricity coursing through me to fire falling on me to angels visiting and much more. This awareness of who you really are is what launches you to be able to walk in both realms at the same time. And when this happens, warfare takes on a whole new dimension.

We will discuss that more in an upcoming chapter. But for now learn the verses that you have chosen. Wear them as a garment and learn to wield them like a sword. Have them ever-ready and on the tip of your tongue.

**Pray and ask God for the spirit of Wisdom and Revelation to come upon you that you might have a greater knowledge and understanding of who you are in Christ and what authority you have been given.

**If you are in a group setting, use the power of agreement as much as you can and pray over each other for Wisdom and Revelation to come. Ask that it be ever increasing as He gives you greater and greater revelation.

3

THE WEAPONS OF OUR WARFARE

For the weapons of our warfare are not carnal, but mighty through God to the pulling down of strongholds.

(2 Corinthians 10:4)

The Lord has given us everything we need in the way of weaponry and help as we engage the enemy. The weaponry of course is spiritual, just like our foe. But don't be thrown by the fact that you don't normally see the weapons the Lord has given us. They are more real and more powerful than anything man could ever dream up.

And our help? The Lord Himself, Holy Spirit, The Father, the angelic host, the cloud of witnesses, the saints, the prophets, and living creatures. God can use whomever He chooses to use. All of Heaven and more is at His disposal .

The Blood of Jesus

And they overcame him through the blood of the Lamb, and by the word of their testimony; and they loved not their lives unto the death. (Revelation 12:11)

In deliverance sessions (where evil spirits are cast out or exorcised from people) nothing seems to torment evil spirits more than hearing about the blood of Jesus.

This seems to weaken them and remove their resolve to resist. This would include scriptures about the blood, songs about the blood, the profession that the person is washed in the blood of the Lamb etc..

Regardless of whether you are dealing with an evil spirit in a person or an evil spirit in a situation, the power of the blood of Jesus cannot be overemphasized. His blood is a mighty weapon of warfare.

I heard a testimony from a former witch who had come to Christ concerning the power of the blood of Jesus. It seems this women's coven had decided to concoct some evil against a little girl who lived across the street from this former witch. Every day however as the little girl would leave for school the mother would "plead" (declare) the blood of Jesus over her daughter. Years later after the witch had gotten saved, she repented to the woman and said "We had tried to harm your little girl but she always had a spiritual covering over her that we could not penetrate." The blood of Jesus was that covering.

There is Power in the Blood

For this is my blood of the covenant, which is poured out for many for the forgiveness of sins. (Matthew 26:28)

The blood of Jesus provides many things for us.

In Him we have redemption through His blood, the forgiveness of sins, in accordance with the riches of God's grace. (Ephesians 1:7)

But if we walk in the light as He is in the light, we have fellowship with one another, and the blood of Jesus Christ His son cleanses us from all sin. (1 John 1:7)

Therefore brethren, having boldness to enter the holiest by the blood of Jesus. (Hebrews 10:19)

Then Jesus said to them, "Most assuredly I say to you, unless you eat the flesh of the son of man and drink His blood, you have no life in you." (John 6:53)

He who eats my flesh and drinks my blood abides in me, and I in him. (John 6:56)

Therefore Jesus also, that He might sanctify the people with His own blood, suffered outside the gate.

(Hebrews 13:12)

All of the things that the Lord Jesus provided through the shedding of His blood must be appropriated by the believer. It's not enough that He did it, (shed His blood) we must accept the provision by faith and apply it to our lives and circumstances.

We Know the Blood of Jesus

One day a friend of mine was grocery shopping when a panhandler approached him and demanded money from him. My friend told the man that he didn't have any money for him and the man began to get more aggressive. Finally it got to the point that my friend thought that he might have to defend himself against the man, so he simply said "The blood of Jesus against you!" The man, backing up began to say in a demonic voice "We know the blood of Jesus." And then the man left the store. They do know the blood of Jesus.

"The blood of Jesus against you!" is a rebuke against the demonic, or any thing or any situation where you may not know immediately what to do.

Applying the Blood of Jesus

All of the weapons in our arsenal such as the blood of Jesus, we apply or use by faith and by a declaration or by speaking or commanding what we desire to happen. It is a normal thing for anyone seated in authority in Christ to be able to command things to come to pass or command situations to change or command something give way to the power of Jesus' blood. Like the word says, "our weapons are not carnal..." we are not swinging a literal sword in the natural but a spiritual sword by declaration. It's more powerful.
To "apply" the blood of Jesus, this is what you should do. First, being aware of the significance of His blood and the power that it holds, you make a declaration or a prayer along these lines...

In Jesus' name, I apply the blood of Jesus over so and so's body. (or life or desires or work or situation) I declare that the blood of Jesus cleanses them now. I declare that the blood of Jesus is a hedge around them that the enemy cannot penetrate.

Remember something here... This is not just you wishing that these things would come to pass. This is not you hoping that the Lord will hear this prayer and have mercy on you and do something! No, this is YOU doing something from the AUTHORITY that JESUS himself gave you to use! As you begin to use His name and His authority you will gain a real sense of the awesome power and authority that He has entrusted to you.

"In Jesus' name, I place the blood of Jesus over every place I go, every building or home I enter, I place the blood of Jesus over my thoughts and desires and emotions. I am covering my family with the blood of Jesus and I am calling for the manifestation of every good thing that His blood purchased for me. I cover my home with the blood of Jesus. I cover my spouse and my marriage with the blood of Jesus."
This is a short example to show you how easy it is to cover your life, family or circumstances with the blood of Jesus. In the chapters ahead I will provide specific examples of how you might pray for very specific things that you are dealing with, such as unsaved loved ones, personal temptations, marriage problems, etc.. Then you can

take from the examples the things that would apply to your own life and build on that.

The Word of Your Testimony

We covered a part of this earlier but there is more to lay hold of with the power of the testimony. A very real part of your testimony is how the Lord rescued you from sin and bondage that you may have been under. You see, a very real thing that can happen in your personal walk is temptations to lure you back into the things that may have held you in the past. The devils are not stupid, they will always go with what has worked in the past. They will arrange scenarios that make it easier for you to fall. It is not hard for them to find someone who is unwittingly willing to help them to make you fall. People are lined up around the block to do the things that make the devil "happy".

In times of rejoicing and in times of sorrow, always give thanks to the Lord for the things He has done for you. This testimony strengthens your being against the lies and temptations he might issue against you.

Suppose that at one time you used to be angry but God delivered you. Now, every day as you realize what God has done for you and how it has blessed you, you give your testimony. When a situation comes up that used to provoke anger, you just thank God.

"Lord, I thank you that I am delivered from anger. I am a new creature in Christ now. The fruit of the Spirit is now manifest in my life, love, joy, peace, patience, kindness, goodness, faithfulness, gentleness and self-control. Anger has no place in me and I thank you Lord."

Now this is important. As you give your testimony, you do acknowledge what God has delivered you from, but you never focus on it. You don't relive it in any way, shape or form. Our focus is always on the things that we desire. What we focus on, we will connect with. This is a powerful spiritual truth. Don't try to relive any of the sins or ungodly scenarios of your past. They are all under the blood. Leave them there.

If the enemy can get you thinking about all the sins and weaknesses of the past, he can more easily bring them into your present and future. If you find yourself thinking about past sins and failures, just say " I rebuke you devil. Get out of my thoughts" and purposely begin to meditate on a favorite scripture or something like that. Don't give him place.

HOW TO DO SPIRITUAL WARFARE

And They Loved Not Their Lives...

And they overcame him by the blood of the Lamb, and by the word of their testimony; and they loved not their lives unto the death. (Revelation 12:11)

Ok, we get the first two but where does that third line fit in when it comes to spiritual warfare? *"And they loved not their lives unto the death."*

In warfare, it is impossible to harm someone who is already dead. When we become alive in Christ we become dead to self. The things that control and manipulate the world, do not manipulate us. We have already laid down our own agenda, our own desires, our own plans etc., and Christ has become everything.

The threats of the enemy have no power at that point.

For me to live is Christ, and to die is gain. (Philippians 1:21)

I realize that for most of us this is still a work in progress. But The Holy Spirit helps us to come into the reality of this scripture and makes it a part of us.

The laying down of the desires of the flesh is a work of sanctification and the Lord is faithful to help us .

It's a process of continually submitting to His will in all things. And when you *know* you are in the middle of God's will, your faith becomes unshakable and even concerning warfare, you have a bold confidence in your relationship with Him.

Binding and Loosing

Binding is the act of tying or wrapping, or to tie the hands or feet to prevent escape or movement. To confine, restrain or restrict as if with bonds. To tie together or to constrain with legal authority. To forbid by indisputable authority.

Loosing is the act of releasing or letting loose. To undo, detach or discharge. To untie or unfetter something or someone. To set free. To permit by indisputable authority.

Verily I say unto you, Whatsoever ye shall bind on earth shall be bound in heaven: and whatsoever ye shall loose on earth shall be loosed in heaven. (Matthew 18:18)

Clearly we see that whatever we bind on earth will be bound in Heaven and whatever we loose on Earth will be loosed in Heaven. But what exactly does this mean for us and how exactly do we accomplish this?

What are the practical steps that make this scripture so important to us?

And I will give unto thee the keys of the kingdom of heaven: and whatsoever thou shalt bind on earth shall be bound in heaven: and whatsoever thou shalt loose on earth shall be loosed in heaven. (Matthew 16:19)

In Matthew chapter sixteen, the Lord is speaking to Peter and the other apostles. To many who are religious but who do not embrace the fact that we have a *supernatural* Gospel, this only means that Jesus was giving the permission to preach the Gospel. But I, as well as many others believe that this commissioning is more encompassing than that. The word "whatsoever" is a *very* open ended word. This was the Lord Jesus giving us His followers Heavenly authority. This authority is vast and powerful and a very useful spiritual weapon. How do I know that this binding and loosing is effective for us today?

On Earth, In Heaven

When the scripture says *"Whatsoever things you bind on earth"* it is speaking of the place where we are. We are on Earth and in the natural realm. (as well as the heavenly realm) We speak or make decrees with our natural voices in the natural realm. But the power of the things we say carry great weight in the spirit realm. The phrase *"shall be bound in Heaven"* is speaking expressly about the spirit realm. Evil spirits are beings that occupy the spirit realm and when we bind them in the natural realm, that authority causes them to be bound in the spirit realm where they are.

If nothing else as you read this book you should lay hold of the fact that you can literally create the reality you live in with the words you speak. God has given us incredible power and authority through the spoken word, to use against the demonic or to use in blessing as well.

Death and life are in the power of the tongue: and they that love it shall eat the fruit thereof. (Proverbs 18:21)

For verily I say unto you, That whosoever shall say unto this mountain, Be thou removed, and be thou cast into the sea; and shall not doubt in his heart, but shall believe that those things which he saith shall come to pass; he shall have whatsoever he saith. (Mark 11:23)

In Mark chapter eleven the Lord makes it clear that you can have what you say. This of course extends over the area of warfare and deliverance as well.

If there is something, some mountain blocking your blessing or your life in some way, speak to that mountain and command it to move.

Please Clarify Your Command

One evening not so long ago, I was doing warfare on behalf of a young man. I had been "binding" the demon who was controlling his behavior. After about maybe an hour or so of this binding, I was suddenly drawn into the spirit realm and found myself standing in front of the demon that I had been binding. This demon was a little larger than me and had a demonic appearance, but I was not in the least afraid or intimidated by him. (by God's grace) The demon then spoke to me. He said.

"Am I bound here, or am I just bound from him?" (referring to the man.)

After this evil spirit asked me this question, I began to have an increased sense of the authority that the Lord has given us and just how specific we could be in using it. Of course I then told the evil spirit that he was bound in every way, that he was not to move, communicate or manifest in any way, shape or form. I then came back out of that realm and realized that my time of warfare was over for the evening and that it had been successful.

** I will explain in greater detail what exactly I did and said concerning this binding I had been doing in the section that addresses specific scenarios.

Binding and Loosing

I also say to you that you are Peter, and upon this rock I will build My Church, and the gates of Hades will not overpower it. I will give you the keys of the Kingdom of Heaven; and whatever you shall bind on earth shall be bound in Heaven, and whatever you shall loose on earth shall be loosed in Heaven. (Matthew 16:18-19)

Binding

We obviously cannot bind someone's freewill. We cannot bind their actions or desires. But we can and do bind the demons that influence them. We also bind the demons and their activities in our lives and in the lives of others and we bind the work of the devil in situations of every kind. I will again provide some basics in this explanation and more specific situations to draw examples from in upcoming chapters.

In utilizing this authority, we again do so through our *speech*. We *say* that which we desire to happen. We command that which we have decided. (Job 22:28)

For instance if you believe that a spirit of anger is afflicting someone you care about you might say,

"Spirit of anger I bind you in Jesus' name" or *"Any spirit causing so and so to feel or be angry, I bind you in Jesus' name"*.

You should probably cover all the bases when you do this. Such as,

"I bind the spirit of anger, or any spirit causing anger in so and so in Jesus' name. I bind all manifestation, communication or transference of this spirit by any means in Jesus' name."

When I do this, I state and restate this in any way I can think of. Let's say the issue is indeed anger (but it could just as well be lust or rebellion or anything else) and I am bringing to bare the authority we have been given. I will bind this spirit and keep binding him until I *feel* a release. There will come a point when the burden to pray or do warfare will lift or significantly lessen. That's when I know I am done. I will then move on to the next issue or begin to praise the Lord for victory.

I also use the binding in a positive way. Such as,

"I bind godly joy to so and so, I bind holiness to my household or I bind myself to the Lord Jesus Christ. I bind the fruit of the spirit to my life and to my family."

List some ways that you might use this in your own life or ministry.

_____
_____
_____
_____
_____
_____
_____
_____
_____
_____
_____
_____
_____

Loosing

Loosing is the act of releasing something by decree (or speech) again, in the natural realm that is then manifested in the spiritual realm.

We can loose the good things of God into our lives and circumstances.

"In Jesus' name, I loose mighty warrior angels to come and fight on our behalf. I loose ministering spirits of God into this situation."

"I loose the spirit of wisdom and revelation. I loose the seven spirits of God. I loose the fruit of the spirit into my life." "I loose clarity and purpose, I loose purity and holiness, I loose the manifest will of God over my life, family and circumstances.'

We can also loose ourselves from bondage or demonic manipulations, from sickness and disease or from any other ungodly trait or affliction.

"I loose myself from every ungodly soul tie. I loose my household from all the power of the enemy. I loose my children from all ungodly words spoken over them or against them. I loose my blessings from the hands or manipulations of the enemy."

When loosing anything I again will do this until I feel a release of some kind. A knowledge that something has been accomplished. Also, Binding and loosing are not exclusive from each other. They should be used together in any situation that you are dealing with.

How might you use "loosing" in your own situations?

_____
_____
_____
_____
_____
_____
_____
_____
_____
_____
_____
_____

Rebuking the Enemy

A rebuke is a stern disapproval or reprimand. To mete out due measure. To censure.

Submit yourselves therefore to God. Resist the devil, and he will flee from you. (James 4:7)

And Jesus rebuked the devil; and he departed out of him: and the child was cured from that very hour. (Matthew 17:18)

When you rebuke the enemy you are meting out a type of judgment against him. You are denying his right to do whatever he is trying to do against you. You are making a statement that you won't put up with it.

Usually I rebuke an evil spirit when I first become aware of his presence in any way.

It seems as if the less time a spirit has been afflicting you, the easier it is to make them go away. If you put up with them being there after you know they are there, it encourages them to hang on because they believe you will eventually stop bothering them. Always try to be quick in your response.

If I suddenly become aware that something just doesn't feel right and there is no logical explanation I rebuke the enemy. *"I rebuke you in Jesus' Name. You are not welcome here and I command you to leave."* If you become aware of an evil spirit in a person, they don't even have to be close by. There is no distance in the spirit realm. *"You evil spirit afflicting _____, I rebuke you in Jesus' name and I bind your power."*

Usually, I get a little angry when I confront devils because I am concerned for their victims. You don't have to yell and scream at them though because your emotions or the level of your voice is not what moves them, your authority in Christ is what moves them. You could whisper your command or even say it in a normal speaking voice if you choose (or even think it) . The power of your command is in Jesus' name.

_____

_____

_____

Praise and Worship in Warfare

But thou art holy, O thou that inhabitest the praises of Israel. (Psalm 22:3)

Praise and worship are awesome "weapons" at our disposal. Praise and worship confuses the enemy. In 2 Chronicles chapter 20 it tells us of Jehoshaphat preparing for battle. On the word of the prophet, he sends the worshippers to march and sing praises to the Lord at the front of the army. We know from this story that the Lord caused their enemies to become confused and they then attacked and destroyed each other. The Lord had completely done the work.

When you worship and praise God, you attract the attention of Heaven. When you love and honor God, He makes his presence manifest in your life and situations. (John 14:21)

When God brings His light to bare it displaces the darkness. This is seen most obviously in the ministry today of those believers who minister "in the glory." There are meetings and church services where the presence of God is so strong that people can hardly handle it.

In those atmospheres, the presence of God is delivering those in bondage and healing the sick as well as other miracles, without anyone being specifically prayed for. Just being in that atmosphere brings the manifestation.

In my own times of warfare and warfare prayer, I like to worship for a time, then do warfare and then back to worship again. It builds up my faith and also brings an atmosphere that makes warfare easier.

It keeps our focus on the fact that our God is all powerful and we can praise Him because He keeps his promises. The enemy stands no chance against our God.

I would suggest praising or singing a praise song about how powerful God is or perhaps singing about the blood of Jesus and the power in the blood. Maybe sing two or three good worship songs before you even start prayer or making decrees etc..

A sword in your hand and God's praises in your mouth!

Let the high praises of God be in their mouth, and a two-edged sword in their hand...
(Psalm 149:6)

_____

_____

_____

Intercession

Intercession is where the incredible stuff happens in my opinion.

The definition of intercession does not convey the full meaning of what I consider it to be.

Intercession: The act of interceding. Prayer, petition, or entreaty in favor of another.

Of course that is the definition of the word but in my own life, because I do believe that we have incredible and undeniable power through Christ, I always see intercession as having accomplished something. If I can redefine the definition with faith I would say that it is the act of interceding with change coming about as the result.

I will tell you a secret about intercession. With the authority of Christ and a heart that says I will allow God to use me in intercession, there is nothing beyond your realm of possibility. No bondage or sickness or demonic foe will withstand you.

I have always believed and seen the reality of this...

If you are willing to pray until you see the breakthrough, you will see the breakthrough.

This is a major place that the enemy has had victory over the saints of God. Most believers grow weary just shy of their victory. I know that sounds cliché but it's true.

Intercession of the magnitude that moves mountains is the kind that will never quit. It's the kind that says I will believe God and look for His victory.

Let me give you a couple examples concerning intercession.

An Evangelist / Pastor was asked to pray for a young girl that was dying of a diseased organ. The girl had perhaps only days to live and the doctors said there was nothing more they could do. The Pastor was led of the Lord to pray for more than a full day continually. This pastor, along with his wife prayed for this girl for more than one full day. When they were done the Lord told them "It is done." The doctors had no explanation but the girl was no longer dying but had a brand new organ. I don't mean that they went about their day while also keeping the girl in prayer. I mean they hit their knees for more than 24 hours praying expressly for this girl.

Not long ago I was also led to fast and pray for an extended period of time for someone who was dying. Although I went about my normal day, I also kept the person in prayer that the Lord led me to pray for. In the evenings I would pray with more focus because that is when I had the time to do so.

I was binding and rebuking sickness, disease and death every day for many days. Although I did not feel any weird manifestations or opposition, the person was delivered. Clean bill of health.

Does it always take such extreme times of prayer and warfare to get a result? This is a question I hear a lot and I don't have a clear concept of what people mean by a lot. A lot is a relative and subjective term. Not long ago the Lord told me to intercede for two hours for someone. I prayed for about twenty minutes, and because it was late and I was tired I told the Lord "Lord, I am too tired to stay up and pray. Can you get someone else?" And then I went to bed. At about one o'clock in the morning I got a phone call to take them to the hospital and ended up staying in the E.R. until about six a.m..

So was two hours of prayer a lot compared to five hours at the ER?

Has the Lord ever asked you to intercede or pray for extended times for a person or a situation? What was the result? We need to keep the record of the victories handy so that we can encourage ourselves as we face other things.

What were some of your times and the result?

1. _____

2. _____

3. _____

4. _____

5. _____

If you are in a group, share some of these testimonies with each other. What were some things the Lord taught you through these experiences?

Faith

Following the subject of intercession, I would like to talk about faith for just a minute.

Now faith is the substance of things hoped for, the evidence of things not seen. (Hebrews 11:1)

Hebrews chapter eleven is the "faith chapter" in the Bible and is a faith builder and encouragement for us. Read it and *expect* God to increase your faith.

When I read books or stories or testimonies of men and women who have or had great faith I see a common thread in them. *Perseverance.* I know we are backtracking a bit but I want To show you something about these people who had such great success in God and in changing the world around them.

A young man in a wheelchair is wheeled up to the front after the service for prayer. Everyone is hoping something will happen, especially the young man. The prayer group anoints him with oil , and lays hands on him and prays the right prayer for a good fifteen minutes. Everyone watches expectantly as the young man tries to get up and walk. But...it just doesn't happen. The young man, discouraged, is wheeled out with the people saying "I really thought I heard God that he would be healed." They will try again next month or maybe in a few months when the healing evangelist comes through. I have to give these people credit because at least they call the sick up to pray for them when they hear God's voice. That alone takes faith! Faith moves! Faith does something!

But what exactly was the problem? Why is it a Smith Wigglesworth or a John G. Lake or a T.L. Osborn were constantly lifting people out of wheelchairs and healing every disease and raising the dead and delivering people from total demonization?

Of course Holiness plays a part, But if you examine their ministries you will see perseverance. Smith Wigglesworth would go into people's homes and pray for hours for them to bring about the healing. John G. Lake would also pray for hours for one healing. I have read many testimonies where these guys prayed for *days* for one healing. T. L. Osborn was praying for the healing of a blind woman once and the healing didn't immediately manifest. He was very surprised. He prayed for that woman every night for the full eight nights of the crusade and on the eighth night the woman, who had been blind most of her life was completely healed and restored." Lord why?" was his question. The Lord showed him in a vision that there was a spirit that looked like an octopus with eight tentacles that had been wrapped around the woman's eye. Every time T.L. prayed. A tentacle was cut off. After all the tentacles had been cut off, she could then see.

Faith is not something we work up or try hard for. Jesus said that faith as a grain of a mustard seed would move mountains.

And Jesus said unto them, Because of your unbelief: for verily I say unto you, If ye have faith as a grain of mustard seed, ye shall say unto this mountain, Remove hence to yonder place; and it shall remove; and nothing shall be impossible unto you.
(Matthew 17:20)

How much faith is that? I believe it is just the faith to actually do it. You know a result is forthcoming because the Word is true. We do not allow ourselves the luxury of discouragement or embarrassment but continue on....in faith!

The Word says that everyone is given a measure of faith.

For I say, through the grace given unto me, to every man that is among you, not to think of himself more highly than he ought to think; but to think soberly, according as God hath dealt to every man the measure of faith. (Romans 12:3)

If you have enough faith to follow the directions given in the Word for manifesting supernatural realities, they will be manifested. Well...now I've gone too far. I have been actually assaulted for saying this to a man once. I don't blame him. He was in pain over an issue and had been "praying" over it for several years. When I told him that, it sounded flippant to him. Like I didn't consider his prayer as real or sincere, and he hit me.

Sometimes when you pray for someone, it looks like nothing is happening. *By faith* you continue anyway. In John G. Lake's healing rooms in Spokane Washington, tens of thousands were healed and the healings were actually documented. Here is how they would do it. A person say with a disease of some sort would come into the healing rooms for prayer. They would pray over the person for one hour and then send them next door to have an x-ray taken. The next day, they would repeat the process, and the next and the next, and so on. In many, many cases there would be absolutely no change for many days. And then.... A slight change in the x-rays....The next one showing even less of the disease. Then less...and less....until the disease was completely gone! You can research the healing rooms and read it for yourself!

Had they used the prayer model of most churches, I don't think they would have had the same success. They had enough *faith to believe the Word and to do it* until it manifested.

That is the kind of faith I am talking about. The Word is true. Do it until it happens.

This is also true in deliverance as well and spiritual warfare.

Many people have strongholds in their lives, many have torments and fears or some sort of addiction. Someone prays for someone else's deliverance and proclaim it done. Many times that is true. There are people walking in that level of power and authority. It wasn't free though, they paid a price for it I guarantee it. Other times the same scenario occurs and the person goes away still in bondage. Why? Because presumption is not faith. Many people want to proclaim it done with a single word because "that's the way Jesus did it." Or "That's the way brother so and so does it and he always has great success doing it that way." However Jesus *and* brother so and so spent incredible amounts of time in the secret place when everybody else was sleeping.

I have similar experiences myself on both ends of the spectrum. There have been times when I have rebuked an evil spirit and nothing happens.

I continue to rebuke the spirit and still nothing happens. (Or rather, nothing *appears* to be happening) Because I do see in the spirit realm at times, I can observe was is going on while this is happening....

Encountering demons

Once I was in intercession and two evil spirits appeared in my room and just stood there looking at me. I rebuked them and continued to rebuke them with them showing no outward reaction of any kind. After about twenty minutes or so, they left.

Another time while I was praying, some evil looking man with big horns sticking out of each side of his head showed up in the room where I was praying. He looked like an eight foot tall, evil man with horns. I rebuked him in every way I knew how and he just looked at me. After about one hour or so, he flew away.

Still yet another time I had been in intercession for several hours when I confronted a rather large demon who made it clear to me that he had a legal right to be where he was because the man I was praying for wanted him there. And that was absolutely true. We can't override someone's free will. We still intercede but not having the same effect it would as for someone who actually wants to be free.

What about the instantly manifested authority?

Well...There have also been times that I "speak and it is done." Let me give an illustration of this as well. I had been praying and fasting for more than a week when I found myself in the spirit realm one night. I encountered an evil spirit there and even though I knew he was a very powerful spirit, I rebuked him and he instantly obeyed me. I spoke a word, and it was done.

Levels

I know you see where I am going with this. There are "levels" it seems. One level is where you use the authority you have been given, by faith and you will see results. Another level is when you walk in a greater anointing because you are constantly making yourself available for God to work through. It gets to the point where every time you encounter that spirit of headache or pain or whatever it happens to be, it is driven out. And then, there is the Glory. People who spend time in the Glory or live or minister in the Glory have that same speak and it is done result. As a matter of fact at that point, when you minister and move in the Glory, you probably won't even have to open your mouth to bring about the deliverance or healing. The power of God to heal will overcome the atmosphere. I am believing for that as well.

The reason the majority of this book is concerning our authority is because that is the level that most believers operate in... For now... But we are being taught to go deeper!

Look at your lives, your church community, your family and see where you are exercising authority continuously to bring about change. Is there anyone in your church who is ill? Is there anyone depressed or discouraged?

Make a list of miracles that you would like to see happen and realize that it will be well worth it to lay hold of your rights and get violent in your authority to see the miracle!

1. _____

2. _____

3. _____

4. _____

5 _____

6 _____

7 _____

8 _____

9 _____

10 _____

What are some of your own experiences with ministry? Have you always had to battle? Do the answers sometimes manifest instantly? Share your victories and failures and talk about possible reasons why.

1. _____

2. _____

3. _____

4. _____

5. _____

6. _____

The Power of Agreement

Again I say unto you, That if two of you shall agree on earth as touching anything that they shall ask, it shall be done for them of my Father which is in heaven. (Matthew 18:19)

For where two or three are gathered together in my name, there am I in the midst of them. (Matthew 18:20)

There is power in a prayer of agreement. If one can put a thousand to flight, two can put ten thousand to flight. (Duet. 32:30) This is something we should take advantage of as much as possible. Not everyone is in the same place spiritually but we can still agree on something that needs to be done and agree that we want God to do it.

Anything you do in the Kingdom, if you have the opportunity for someone to come into agreement with you, do it. This is especially powerful for families, husbands and wives, children, church families etc.. Use this resource that the Lord has given and you will see that the results will be forthcoming! If you don't have a spouse that is believing or willing, a good friend can make a powerful prayer partner.

Another Three Fold Cord

Prayer

Confess your faults one to another, and pray one for another, that ye may be healed. The effectual fervent prayer of a righteous man availeth much. (James 5:16)

But when ye pray, use not vain repetitions, as the heathen do: for they think that they shall be heard for their much speaking. (Matthew 6:7)

As you engage in warfare for deliverance or healing or the change of circumstances, you will see what works and what doesn't. For example "rote" prayers will not work in general, but they will work if that is the only "light" that you have. Just the fact that you bring your needs to the Lord will be enough even if you don't know all the right words on your own.

But prayer is the most powerful thing you can ever do in this world to change or influence anything. Pray real prayers from your heart. Don't posture or try to put on airs just make your requests known to God and know that He hears you.

Fasting

"And when you fast, do not look gloomy like the hypocrites, for they disfigure their faces that their fasting may be seen by others. Truly, I say to you, they have received their reward. But when you fast, anoint your head and wash your face, that your fasting may not be seen by others but by your Father who is in secret. And your Father who sees in secret will reward you. (Matthew 6;16-18)

"Is not this the fast that I choose: to loose the bonds of wickedness, to undo the straps of the yoke, to let the oppressed[b] go free, and to break every yoke? (Isaiah 58:6)

Really, the entire chapter of Isaiah fifty eight is a helpful guide. Fasting is a way of humbling yourself. It is a way of denying your flesh so that your spirit man has full reign for whatever reason or task at hand. Anytime you seek to access spiritual realities, gifts, fruits of the spirit etc., fasting is a way to clear the clutter. In conjunction with prayer it takes things to a new level.

One of the most phenomenal deliverances the Lord has ever used me for occurred at the end of a fast. If you have never tried it, I would encourage you to do so.

Giving

How does giving figure into a three -fold chord? Because giving is an act of obedience. Sometimes we don't want to hear about that because of all the TV preachers we have heard who have the same word of knowledge every week about you sowing into their ministry. That does not negate the principle nor the reality however.

Every man according as he purposeth in his heart, so let him give; not grudgingly, or of necessity: for God loveth a cheerful giver. And God is able to make all grace abound toward you; that ye, always having all sufficiency in all things, may abound to every good work: (2 Corinthians 9:7,8)

It does seem like every time I hear a message on giving or sowing seed it has to do with financial prosperity or getting something financial from the Lord. But some of the greatest blessings the Lord has given me through sowing had nothing to do with money, but rather obedience on my part and the yield was something money could not buy.

I can't give the details of this particular testimony but I would still like to convey as much as I can because of the element of giving. I had been praying for something serious and personal for several months., believing the Lord to do something big on my behalf. In the midst of this time, I suddenly heard God say that He wanted me to sow a rather large seed. At the time, I did not see any relation between the two.

The Lord then supernaturally actually gave me the seed to sow. (This has happened many times and I encourage you too, to ask the Lord to give you seed to sow) At the time it was the largest amount I had ever sown at one time. But, since I clearly heard His voice and He did actually give me the seed also, I sowed it. I did not know what the purpose was.

Within two weeks of having sown the seed, one of the major breakthroughs of my life manifested and has altered the course of my family. It is powerful.

Prayer, fasting and giving, a powerful three fold cord.

Think of the times you have fasted and prayed. What was Heaven's reaction? Can you trace any blessings from God to seeds you have sown? What are they?

1. _____

2. _____

3. _____

4. _____

5. _____

There were a lot of topics covered in this chapter. Things that are vital in spiritual warfare. Ask the holy Spirit to give you great clarity in using the weapons of warfare and that He would make it natural to you.

4

THE WHOLE ARMOR OF GOD

Put on the whole armour of God, that ye may be able to stand against the wiles of the devil. (Ephesians 6:11)

The whole armor of God is the thing most talked about when you hear a sermon on spiritual warfare. I love to hear this topic preached on because this is one area that is important to me.

Be strong in the Lord and in his mighty power. Put on the full armour of God so that you can take your stand against the devil's schemes. For our struggle is not against flesh and blood, but against the rulers, against the authorities, against the powers of this dark world and against the spiritual forces of evil in the heavenly realms. Therefore put on the full armour of God, so that when the day of evil comes, you may be able to stand your ground, and after you have done everything to stand. Stand firm then, with the belt of truth buckled round your waist, with the breastplate of righteousness in place, and with your feet fitted with the readiness that comes from the gospel of peace. In addition to all this, take up the shield of faith, with which you can extinguish all the flaming arrows of the evil one. Take the helmet of salvation and the sword of the Spirit, which is the word of God. (Ephesians 6:10-17)

To start things off on the right foot, I would like to state that the whole armor of God is a supernatural reality. The majority of messages you will hear of this subject will present the armor by using natural explanations for this supernatural reality. So I want to jump out here and say that I have seen this armor in the spirit realm and it is *real*. It is not some analogy to make a point or a metaphor to make the point stick in your mind. No, the whole armor is a real spiritual thing.

The first thing that I would suggest is that even before you understand fully about the whole armor, you begin to lay hold of it by faith. Here is how I do it.

Dear Lord, Right now by faith I take hold of your provision for warfare and protection, the whole armor of God. I put on the helmet of salvation. I put on the breastplate of righteousness. I wrap around my loins the girdle of truth. I put upon my feet the shoes of the preparation of the gospel of peace. I take the shield of faith by which every fiery dart Is quenched and I take up the sword of the spirit which is the word of God. Lord teach me about this armor. Let the reality of this armor be manifest in my life. Make me a soldier that is effective for the sake of the Kingdom. In Jesus' name, amen. "

Stand therefore, having your loins girt about with truth, and having on the breastplate of righteousness; (Ephesians 6:14)

Loins gird about with truth

Truth is foundational in the life of a Christian. You can't walk in power and in a lie at the same time. Satan is the father of lies. The enemy will try to get you to lie in the course of your life because if you walk in mixture, you will have very little power in the spiritual realm. Oh it won't be anything big, but then again it doesn't have to be. "Tell them I'm not home" or "The check is in the mail" or "I'm too sick to come in" (cough, cough) Just enough mixture that that part of your armor is spoiled.

Truth is also foundational in the area of the scriptures themselves and correct interpretation and application of them for our lives. Scriptures that have been dumbed down for instance, will not convey the correct or truthful meaning and will not have the power to work in your life.

This is one area of pet peeve for me. It never ceases to amaze me that people can take the most supernatural verses in the Bible and say "well...that's not *really* what it means."

Wherefore putting away lying, speak every man truth with his neighbor: for we are members one of another. (Ephesians 4:25)

Lie not one to another, seeing that ye have put off the old man with his deeds; (Colossians 3:9)

Of course we must speak the truth **in love.** If love is not our motivation we shouldn't speak. I had a friend once that would say the most ungodly, horrendous things and when I would call him on them his excuse was always that he was bound to speak the truth. I don't think that's what God had in mind.

If you purpose to walk in the truth, it will be easier to walk in the truth...and in love.

The Breastplate of Righteousness

Our own righteousness is as filthy rags but thankfully Jesus gave us His righteousness and took upon Himself our sin.

No weapon that is formed against thee shall prosper; and every tongue that shall rise against thee in judgment thou shalt condemn. This is the heritage of the servants of the LORD, and their righteousness is of me, saith the LORD. (Isaiah 54:17)

And be found in him, not having mine own righteousness, which is of the law, but that which is through the faith of Christ, the righteousness which is of God by faith: (Philippians 3:9)

Righteousness is to be free from guilt or sin or to act fairly according to divine law. To walk in righteousness is to make correct moral judgments. Not being influenced by sin or deceptions. As you study the Word and as the mind of Christ is made manifest within you, the result of Christ's righteousness is all the more evident.

Our Gospel Shoes

And your feet shod with the preparation of the gospel of peace; (Ephesians 6:15)

Our whole mission is the Gospel so it is no wonder that it is part of our armor. The fact that our feet are shod with it I believe is because we take the Gospel everywhere we go, everywhere we travel.

And how shall they preach, except they be sent? as it is written, How beautiful are the feet of them that preach the gospel of peace, and bring glad tidings of good things! (Romans 10:15)

How beautiful upon the mountains are the feet of him that bringeth good tidings, that publisheth peace; that bringeth good tidings of good, that publisheth salvation; that saith unto Zion, Thy God reigneth! (Isaiah 52:7)

I believe also that the shoes denote that the Gospel gives us a firm footing or foundation. The more we immerse ourselves in the Gospel the more secure our stand will be. If you are swinging a sword around you will need a secure footing.

The Helmet of Salvation

And take the helmet of salvation, and the sword of the Spirit, which is the word of God: (Ephesians 6:17)

I believe that the helmet of salvation is Christ. Christ is our salvation. He is the head of the body, the head of the church and we are also instructed to have the mind of Christ.

Let this mind be in you, which was also in Christ Jesus: (Philippians 2:5)

With Christ as your head and as your covering it will be hard to be swayed in your thinking. The things of the world will not draw your thoughts nor your attentions or affections.

The Sword of the Spirit

The sword of the spirit is the Word of God. That is our weapon. Speaking forth the Word of God is the most powerful thing you can do; the most powerful response you can have. Even the decrees and pronouncements, the praises and the rebukes are based in the Word of God.

You don't need another weapon. That's why the Word says that life and death are in the power of the tongue...

Death and life are in the power of the tongue: and they that love it shall eat the fruit thereof. (Proverbs 18:21)

And he hath made my mouth like a sharp sword; in the shadow of his hand hath he hid me, and made me a polished shaft; in his quiver hath he hid me; (Isaiah 49:2)

For the word of God is quick, and powerful, and sharper than any two-edged sword, piercing even to the dividing asunder of soul and spirit, and of the joints and marrow, and is a discerner of the thoughts and intents of the heart. (Hebrews 4:12)

The sword of the spirit can immediately quench evil thoughts or temptations, it can stop the workings of evil spirits in people or situations. The sword of the spirit can help carve out a victorious life in Christ for you and for others. Keep your sword handy!

The Shield of Faith

Above all, taking the shield of faith, wherewith ye shall be able to quench all the fiery darts of the wicked. (Ephesians 6:16)

Back in the days before I believed in the supernatural things of God, I would see a verse like this and think it meant something like, have faith because that would help us not to give in to the temptation of sin. That the darts were really just temptations to think bad thoughts etc.. Since my spiritual eyes have been opened however, I have actually seen things "stuck" into me in the spirit. They were things that didn't belong and I had to remove. I also saw at one occasion several angry evil spirits that were throwing what appeared to be shards of glass at me. I did not realize it at the time but some of them stuck me and I found them lodged in my feet about two years later and I immediately knew what they were and where they came from. That's one reason I say without hesitation that these weapons and these armors are real spiritual things a that we appropriate by faith and they are powerful.

We wait in hope for the Lord; he is our help and our shield. (Psalms 33:20)

Every word of God is pure: he is a shield unto them that put their trust in him. (Proverbs 30:5)

The shield of faith is believing the things that are truth rather than the bad report or the things that are seen. The things that are seen are subject to change and will give way to the greater spiritual reality when your faith is exercised.

Using the shield of faith is when the medical experts say it's too late there is no hope, but we believe Isaiah fifty three- five instead and declare it over the situation. *"By His stripes we are healed."*

Or when loved ones tell you they will never accept your religion (cause that's what they believe it to be) But you calmly declare *"And they said, Believe on the Lord Jesus Christ, and thou shalt be saved, and thy house." (Acts 16:31)*

What are you own feelings and thoughts about the whole armor of God? How do you appropriate these things for your own lives? What can you share about them that would help others in their own battles and warfare?

_____

_____

_____

_____

_____

_____

_____

_____

_____

_____

_____

_____

_____

_____

_____

_____

_____

_____

_____

In Ephesians chapter six, Paul really makes it clear that this is a spiritual reality and that it is coming. There is no "just in case" mentality here but a surety that the "evil day" will come. All of the armor is given us to deal specifically with the enemy we will face and the kinds of weaponry we will face.

Pray that the Lord will give you greater understanding about the whole armor of God. Pray that it will not just be a written scripture to you but a real and living spiritual reality.

5

WARFARE

Be sober, be vigilant; because your adversary the devil, as a roaring lion, walketh about, seeking whom he may devour: (1 Peter 5:8)

In contemplating how to present this material I had several options. I chose to present the information in a way that it would be instantly useable. The methods, prayers, tactics etc., will be presented in a way that address a particular issue. I feel that this way one can see how the information is used in real life. I didn't want to throw a lot of information at you and then leave you to figure out how it works or how to use it.

Authority, Anointing, and The Glory

The majority of believers that believe in or do spiritual warfare, do it from the place of **authority**. We have been given authority in God's word over unclean spirits and so we act on that authority. There is nothing that can stand against this authority. The Lord has given us authority over *all* the works of the devil. (Luke 10:19) Here I will summarize what I alluded to in an earlier chapter.

And these signs shall follow them that believe; In my name shall they cast out devils; They shall take up serpents; and if they drink any deadly thing, it shall not hurt them; they shall lay hands on the sick, and they shall recover. they shall speak with new tongues; (Mark 16:17, 18)

And the seventy returned again with joy, saying, Lord, even the devils are subject unto us through thy name. (Luke 10:17)

Because the seventy returned with joy saying that the demons were subject to them, I detect that maybe it took them a little by surprise. This is what I would consider operating in the authority of the believer. Jesus said we are to do it, so we can do it.

The anointing, I believe is a particular grace to operate at a higher level of power or authority. Not everyone agrees exactly what the anointing is, but the general idea is that God's power is upon you for a purpose. The power of the Holy Spirit upon you for a particular thing. Such as someone has a strong "healing anointing" or "teaching anointing" etc.. Therefore if a person had a particular anointing in deliverance or healing, then every time they came up against a particular sickness or spirit it would be defeated . This might be manifest in someone who does a lot of spiritual warfare or someone who ministers in the gifts in an ongoing basis.

The Glory is the far end of this spectrum. The person who spends considerable time in God's manifest presence or in the Glory, ministers in a way that is amazing to watch. I say "ministers" but the truth is that just because the person is in the room, and they have the presence of God upon them, people will be healed or delivered many times without a word being spoken. Demons will cry out in reaction to that presence whether a person is seeking deliverance or not. In my opinion this is the place we should all aspire to. We should desire to be in God's presence and carry to it with us everywhere we go. This is the model Jesus gave us. The spirit without measure. This is the level where you would say "Come out in Jesus' name" one time and move on to the next person because there is no doubt whatsoever. I have seen many people who want to emulate the model of Jesus without emulating the life of Jesus. That level of power is not free. I don't mean that you have to pay money for it, but rather you pay with your life. A life abandoned to God in prayer and fasting and waiting on God and studying His word is the price I am taking about. I pray that you do seek this life of the presence of God.

But even if you do not, we don't want the enemy to defeat us or afflict us so we operate from where we are. Don't wait until you can cast out demons like Benny Hinn. Start where you are and you will be successful. God gives "on the job" training.

Personal Warfare

The area most books about warfare address more than any is the area of personal walk or personal holiness. How to counter the wiles of the devil so that a person can have a victorious Christian life. I think that area is important as well, so I will start with that. This area is important for a number of reasons. Two very big ones are , if you can't or don't know how to fight for yourself, you probably won't be able to help anyone else. And B, if you don't fight for yourself you probably won't want to help anyone else. Personal warfare helps you to walk in victory.

First and foremost, A steady and consistent prayer life with study of the Word of God is paramount to living a Godly life and living in victory. If you feel defeated or even low, increase your Bible reading and increase your prayer time and waiting on God.

I was in a personal "dry time" last year and I decided to read ten chapters in the Psalms and shake myself out of it. For me at the time, ten chapters was a lot because I was reading a couple chapters a day. Having read the ten chapters, I felt really good. Later that night when I went to bed, I laid down to some of the most spectacular visions I 'd had in a while! Give God something to work with. Keep the sanctification process going through the Word and prayer.

Temptation

Let's start with temptation, sin and repentance. Here is a foundation for walking in holiness and in the spirit. For quick recovery and getting back on track if you sin.

Where a lot of Christians get defeated and wind up in a perpetual struggle with sin is in focusing on the sin they did and then listening to and accepting the devil's opinion of them about it. It's discouraging. Here is something the Lord taught me about repentance.

If you sin, immediately repent. I mean *immediately.* Even if you have only sinned seconds ago, repent! You say *"well I don't feel like it would be sincere."* You need to think about what you have done, focus on it for a while, feel sorry for having done it and then repent. First of all, if you weren't really sorry, you would never even consider repenting. Your soul may not be on board yet, but your spirit wants to repent *now* and get back to where things should be.

Immediate repentance is the first action. Then immediately state your decree about who you really are. That is where your focus should be. You do have to truly repent but you can't wallow in it. If you do the devil will play that game as long as you are willing.

Brethren, I count not myself to have apprehended: but this one thing I do, forgetting those things which are behind, and reaching forth unto those things which are before, I press toward the mark for the prize of the high calling of God in Christ Jesus. (Philippians 3:13, 14)

Train yourself to repent quickly if you sin and get back on track. If you want to walk in the power of God, you have to keep your focus on who you are, not who you were.

Example

I have just sinned. I got angry seemingly for no reason and said some unkind and hurtful things to someone. I knew as soon as the words came out of my mouth that I should not have said them and my flesh is still a little riled but I (my spirit) forces my flesh to apologize and I immediately do so. *"Lord, I am sorry for being angry and unkind, and for saying the things I said. I repent. I won't do it again."* However I continue..."*anger, I do not accept you. You are not a part of me and you never will be. I reject you. I am a son of the most high and you have no place in me."*

Always keep your focus on *who you are in Christ.*

Self- Deliverance

Many times we are not faced with the occasional temptation to sin, but rather an ongoing battle that we seem to be on the losing end of. This is due to some spirit / bondage that we may or may not have let into our lives. Driving thoughts, actions or desires that we can't seem to control. Many people do not have an issue with living this way but to a believer that truly desires to live for God, this is pure torment.

For the record, I do not split hairs about where the spirit is located. (In me, on me, near me, far from me, behind me,) to me that is mostly semantics. If someone I consider trustworthy says *"Mike I see a spirit has somehow gained entrance into you, may I cast it out?"* My answer would always be *"Yes."* I do know that it matters sometimes but usually not in the way most people think. You cannot try to make a distinction like this because of pride or to deny a reality for some reason. The important thing is that we are driving it away. (However, we must be *sensitive* in dealing with others in this regard.)

Regardless of what the sin or bondage is, make a list of all of its' manifestations. What exactly is the tormenting action or thought etc.. Let's say it is lust. Lust is also a big field but because of the culture and its permissive attitude toward sexuality etc., let's narrow it to sexual lust. Let's say that this lust manifests as unclean thoughts, unclean desires, lustful thoughts and desires, and ungodly fantasies and daydreams. The thoughts are driving and tormenting and you want them to stop.

The first steps I always take in deliverance are **repentance** and **forgiveness**. Repent of any sins and make sure you are not in un-forgiveness toward anyone.

Repentance

Repentance breaks a legal right a spirit has to be a part of your life. You may have been in agreement with the unclean spirit in the past, but now you have repented. You no longer are. Forgiveness because more people stay in bondage of every kind due to lack of forgiveness. This is a huge deal in the spirit realm. If there are people you won't forgive, you are only hurting yourself. Many times a deliverance is immediately manifested once the person forgives someone they had previously held something against.

Forgiveness

The scriptures talk about being turned over to the tormentors for not forgiving a debt.

Then came Peter to him, and said, *"Lord, how oft shall my brother sin against me, and I forgive him? til seven times?"* Jesus saith unto him, *'I say not unto thee, Until seven times: but Until seventy times seven. Therefore is the kingdom of heaven like unto a certain king, which would take account of his servants.' "*

"And when he had begun to reckon, one was brought unto him which owed him ten thousand talents (101 million dollars). But forasmuch as he had not to pay, his lord commanded him to be sold, and his wife and his children, and all that he had, and payment to be made. The servant therefore fell down, and worshipped him saying, "Lord, have patience with me, and I will pay thee all." Then the Lord of that servant was moved with compassion, AND LOOSED HIM AND FORGAVE him the debt."

"But the same servant went out, and found one of his fellow servants, which had owed him an hundred pence: ($44.00), and he laid his hands on his throat, saying, "Pay me that thou owest." And his fellow servant fell down at his feet, and begged him, saying, have patience with me, and I will pay thee all. And he would not: but went and cast him into prison, till he should pay the debt."

"So when his fellow servants saw what was done, they were very sorry, and came and told their lord all that was done. Then his lord after that he had called him, said unto him. O THOU WICKED SERVANT, I FORGAVE THEE ALL THAT DEBT, BECAUSE THOU DESIREDST ME, SHOULD NOT THOU ALSO HAVE HAD COMPASSION ON THEY FELLOW SERVANT, EVEN AS I HAD PITY ON THEE? And his lord was wroth, and DELIVERED HIM TO THE TORMENTORS, till he should pay all that was due unto him."

" So likewise shall my heavenly Father do also unto you, if ye from your hearts forgive not everyone his brother their trespasses."

We have to forgive. It is not an option.

Let's say I've made my list and I have all the issues written down. Now I would begin to address these things in this manner...

In Jesus' name I place myself under the blood of Jesus. I place my spirit, soul and body under the blood of Jesus. I bind the spirit of ___(lustful dreams)_____ and I command you to go. I bind all communication, manifestation and transference of evil spirits in and around my life. From my position in Christ at God's own right hand I bind you and cast you out. Right now.

And because most spirits leave through breath, I would stop talking a minute, take a few deep breaths and then continue.

You spirit of _____(perversion)_____ I bind you in Jesus' name and I command you to go. Get out in Jesus name. You have no place in me and no power over me. Get out.

Continue through your list and continue with your commands until the deliverance is manifest. (they leave)

Then after you stop ask the Holy Spirit to fill you with His holy presence and take back all the area of your life that had previously been afflicted.

"Holy Spirit, fill me now with your holy presence. Fill all the areas of my life. I give myself to you completely. Redeem and fill every part of me, spirit, soul and body. Make me holy and help me to walk in holiness. In Jesus' name. Amen."

Maybe your issue is fear or tiredness or maybe it's laughing at inappropriate jokes or whatever. Make your list and exhaust all possible manifestations and then pray through that list. But Mike, what if the thing turns out to be just a physical affliction or some desire of the flesh? Well... no harm then. The name of Jesus is still above a natural carnal desire or physical affliction. It must still yield to the name of Jesus. So you haven't lost anything. Better safe than sorry especially if you have been praying over an issue for a long time and seeing no results.

It is also important to ask the Holy Spirit and allow Him to tell you things about what you are praying about. Ask for words of knowledge. A word of knowledge that exposes a spirit can instantly break their power and drive them out!

You can also use a book that gives listing of grouping of devils that seem to work together. Go through the list in relation to yourself (or whoever you are praying for) and you can be sure to cover all the bases.

I know what you are thinking...Christians with such demonic problems? Really?

How many of you know people who have personalities that go a little "south" sometimes? Brother so and so is usually so nice but he is acting *almost* demonic. Sister so and so always says such hurtful things or Sister so and so's family has always had a lot of headaches... etc., etc..

If I start to feel a little funny, or I feel that I have been "slimed" somehow, I will practice this self-deliverance. And I have gotten relief many times.

Our Families

I am going to present some of the most common scenarios surrounding family issues and how I would, or do deal with them.

Marriage

This is an area that the enemy loves to attack for a couple of reasons. God loves families and God instituted marriage. Plus an unstable marriage allows a host of other problems in to afflict the rest of the family. To anyone who has experienced strife in their marriage, you know exactly what I'm saying and that this is true.

Many a man claims to have unfailing love, but a faithful man who can find? The righteous man leads a blameless life; blessed are his children after him.
(Proverbs 20: 6,7)

A wife of noble character who can find? She is worth far more than rubies.
(Proverbs 31:10)

What are some of the things the enemy can bring into a home where the marriage relationship is rocky?

1. _____

2. _____

3. _____

4. _____

5. _____

6. _____

7. _____

I'm going to lead on this one with a confession. An actual example from my own life just to get the ball rolling. I had been complaining to the Lord for some time actually about my wife. *"Lord why isn't she nicer to me? Why doesn't she make me meat loaf anymore? I am such a hard worker why won't she rub my feet more? Why doesn't she seem happy with me?'* I had a long list of complaints that I brought to the Lord of which I only told you four. This complaining went on for quite a while actually. I wasn't so much asking the Lord for answers, I was telling Him that He wasn't being fair with me. I deserved better.

One day (and it took way too long for me to get there) I *sincerely* asked the Lord for a real answer to my complaints. He responded instantly. He said *"Mike, you have provided no prayer covering for your wife. She is virtually unprotected except for my grace. You are allowing the enemy to torment her and you are not doing the job of priest of your home. It is entirely your fault."*

Ouch! *It was true!* I wasn't lifting her up in prayer! I wasn't pleading the blood of Jesus over her every day! I wasn't binding the work of the enemy against her! I wasn't releasing joy over her! I was only thinking of my own needs and desires with no regard to what was happening to her. I had left her to fend for herself. I am getting emotional even as I write this because it was so selfish and wrong.

Take account of your own relationships. Are you the defender of those the Lord has placed in your charge? Do you pray over them every day? What could you do better? How much of your time are you willing to sacrifice on behalf of them? Make a list and write some real, honest answers. Are your efforts purposeful or haphazard?

1. _____

2. _____

3. _____

4. _____

5. _____

6. _____

7. _____

8. _____

This isn't a male issue. Wives should pray for their husbands as well It's a team effort.

A common goal or direction

A way that we can defeat the enemy in our marriages is by having a common goal that we are pursuing. The Lord. If we are both following the Lord sincerely, it will take a lot of the possible drama out of the relationship. The things that most people in the world face that tear marriages apart are addressed in the Bible and it makes things a non-issue for those who belong to the Lord. Physical or emotional adultery would not be an issue for instance if both are seeking God. It takes a lot of the pressure off to have the answers in advance. But even in that, we still face problems that challenge us.

A Song of degrees for Solomon. Except the LORD build the house, they labour in vain that build it: except the LORD keep the city, the watchman waketh but in vain. (Psalms 127:1)

A covering prayer

Here is a prayer that I pray over my wife and "kids" every day. If it seems a bit over the top, it is only because I have seen spiritual realities and I know how powerful our words are. You can literally create the atmosphere of your home. I will leave the names blank so you can use it if you like.

Father, please forgive me of any sins I may have done. Right now I lift up my family before you. I plead the blood of Jesus over _____ and _____ and _____. I plead the blood of Jesus over their bodies, souls and spirits. I plead the blood of Jesus over their mind, will, emotions, personalities, thoughts, dreams and desires. I plead the blood of Jesus over their memories and imaginations. I plead the blood of Jesus over their past, present and future.

I plead the blood of Jesus over everything they are and everything they have. I plead the blood of Jesus over the vehicles they drive and ride in. I plead the blood of Jesus over the roads and places they travel and the traffic and things around them. I plead the blood of Jesus over their work places, _____, _____ and _____, _____ and _____.

I place their entire beings within the light of your glory Lord. Let a bubble of your glory surround them and protect them. I place them under the angelic canopy. Let the angels of the Lord do everything in their power to manifest the will and the Word of God in their lives. I place their ministries, gifts and callings all under the blood of Jesus. I place their anointings and mantles under the blood of Jesus. I command light to shine upon their path. I release joy and hope and agape love over them. I release kindness, gentleness and meekness over them. I decree that God's plan be manifested in their lives. Father let your Kingdom truly come and your will be done.

That is a shortened version of my prayer over my family. Usually I will pray along these lines for about fifteen minutes or so, also declaring scriptures over my family or specific things as I am led of the Lord. After I have engaged Heaven I also address the evil one.

I bind all the power of the enemy over my family in Jesus name. I bind every strongman, or ruling spirit and I bind every evil spirit and evil being. I bind your ability to communicate, transfer or manifest in any way. You are bound. I command every blocking and hindering spirit to go in Jesus' name. I command all sickness, disease and infirmity to go in Jesus' name. I decree destruction upon all the work of the enemy against us. I command the work of the enemy be as dust beneath the Lord's feet. I command that they be scattered eight ways. I release the lightnings of God against them in Jesus' name. I thank you Lord for complete freedom in the Holy Spirit.

I also follow the voice of the Holy Spirit in this part. And then I will spend some time thanking the Lord for all of His blessings and His mercy and goodness. And then possibly pray in tongues for a while.

The entire "prayer / warfare / praise" I do every morning, and it takes me about thirty to forty five minutes. I do this as I get ready for work and while I am driving to work. For years I would listen to the radio as I drove but I spend more of that time in prayer now than I used to.

Make a list of your own to build into a prayer. What are the areas and people you want to lift up?

1. _____

2. _____

3. _____

4. _____

5. _____

6. _____

If you do this type of covering prayer every day, you will see results. These prayers have their basis in the scriptures and as such they are legal rights that I am claiming over my family. Do this for a month and you will have a different atmosphere in your home. Provide protection to the degree that you have been given the power and authority to do so. Your family will have an increase in the peace that passes understanding.

Our Homes

Our homes should be a safe haven for our families. They should be full to overflowing of the presence and the peace of God. I have seen some Christian homes that have such peace it is *supernatural* and others that seem to have the chaos of the world manifesting in it even though the people genuinely love the Lord. What gives?

Here again we are stewards of our homes. We can set the standard and enforce and maintain it. It is a conscious choice we make or we can leave it to "chance" and hope that God will correct our home life without our having to be involved. Fortunately, or unfortunately God is not an absentee Father. He is not forcing us to do something we don't want to do but He will train us to grow up and become the power heirs that we are.

The enemy will invade our homes if he can because that is the area that we most often relax and let our hair down. If our defenses are down, he can slip in and wreak havoc. How does he do this? There are many things to be aware of.

What are the ways that you think the enemy can sneak into our homes?

_____

_____

_____

_____

_____

People

The things of the world can slip in in the most innocuous ways. Our friends and their influence are a great tool that the enemy can use. The Bible speaks clearly about who we should have fellowship with.

Be ye not unequally yoked together with unbelievers: for what fellowship hath righteousness with unrighteousness? and what communion hath light with darkness? (2 Corinthians 6:14)

And have no fellowship with the unfruitful works of darkness, but rather reprove them. (Ephesians 5:11)

But what about people we have to be around or people we love and are trying to lead to Christ? Yes, that is a legitimate concern. My wife and I were given the answer by the Lord one evening as we were discussing and praying over this very issue. The Lord gave us Psalm 101. It cleared everything up for us. I believe the Lord is saying that we should avoid fellowship with wicked people who claim to be believers.

I don't fault unbelievers for not being Christ-like.

I had a friend once who would come to our house to visit and by the time he left, there was very little peace. The "life" had been sucked out of everyone. The world might call them "high maintenance" people. He might spend thirty minutes talking about how great the Lord is and then give a five second innuendo or unclean statement of some kind. Then talk about the gifts of the Holy Spirit and then utter a curse word. Of course then he would apologize..."*I don't know why I said that. I'm so sorry*" And it would be that way every time. There was a spiritual dynamic going on that was warfare and for a long time I never even realized it. Think carefully and pray about the people you bring into your home for fellowship. Enforce your standard. (with love)

If you are bringing anyone under your roof for any reason, pray over it and plead the power of the blood of Jesus over the situation or visit.

Dear Lord, I lift up our visit with _____ today. I place them and the entire visit under the blood of Jesus. From the moment they step onto our property, let the blood of Jesus cover them and every part of their lives. I bind all of the work of the enemy in and around them and their lives. I bind every evil spirit and their influence in Jesus' name. I bind all manifestation, communication and transference of evil spirits in Jesus' name. Let the presence of God be manifest here and the power of the Kingdom on display. That your name might be glorified. In Jesus' name, amen.

Things

Objects and **items** that we bring into our homes can open spiritual doors for the enemy top afflict us. This is such a big one also because so much of the world has crept into Christian culture. Kind of like, "*we have our normal life, but we are Christian.*" Let me be the first to tell you if you haven't heard the news. We are anything but *normal*. Our standards should reflect the reality of that.

If there is any strange occurrence or shift in the atmosphere in your home that you can't explain, see if there is an object they may have come into your home at the same time. Ask the Holy Spirit of course and listen to His voice. He will show you. A relative recently told us that her young son was suddenly terrified to go into his room and refused to stay in there and go to sleep. He was sleeping with them until they sorted it out. My mom Cathy, asked "*Was anything different about his room now, as opposed to before?*" And she was told yes, that a beautiful baby crib had just been given to them and they put it in his room just before all this started. My mom said "*take it out of the room and go throw it in the trash dumpster.*" And so they did. And guess what? There was no more fear of that room anymore. He began immediately to sleep just fine.

Be aware of what is brought into your home. **Movies** are a good example of how the spiritual atmosphere in your home can be affected. I heard from a minister once that she was shown that when you watch a movie you are not just receiving the sounds and images of the movie, but also the spirit behind the movie from which it was created. I believe that whole heartedly.

I used to hear newscasts where they would report on some young child seven or eight years old, doing the most horrific and ungodly crimes or acts. I would wonder *"What in the world had their parents been letting them watch that they would even think or know to do something like that?"* I found out later that a child does not have to be directly exposed to be afflicted. I have personally seen small children manifest the outward workings of the "secret" sins of the parents. If you bring something evil or unclean into your house, you are giving permission for that spirit to be in your house. They will have a legal right to be there because they were invited in.

Here is another example from my own life....

It was close to midnight and my wife Gordana had already put the kids to bed and gone to bed herself. I had stayed up to relax, drink coffee and watch TV in the garage / family room for a while. For the most part I was watching Christian TV but on occasion I would channel surf to see what else was on. I just happened to come across a popular werewolf movie that had just come out on TV, and I watched it for a few minutes. I began to feel convicted for watching though because of the sheer wickedness of the "hero" of the film, so I changed the channel. However, ten minutes later I again began to watch the show and again felt the conviction of the Holy Spirit and again changed the channel.

You would think that I would have gotten a clue, but no. A little later I once again turned back to the werewolf movie and began watching it. This time, after just a couple of minutes I heard a blood curdling scream coming from the far end of the house from my daughter's room. I ran to her room and found her terrified, cowering and crying. She kept screaming "There's a wolf in my room! There's a wolf in my room!"

You could literally feel the evil presence in the room. I felt very, very low at having subjected my daughter to demonic attack because of my disobedience and I repented profusely. Repentance was a starting place but it still took about two hours of prayer to drive out the evil presence and restore enough peace to my daughter so that she could sleep. I had opened the hedge of protection.

My daughter had not seen or heard any of the movie. She had been asleep. Do not bring anything into your home that you would be embarrassed for Jesus to sit there on the couch and watch with you. The same goes for music and anything else.

Sometimes there are *things that seem totally innocent* that we bring in. It has nothing to do with any bad choices or sins. We have to be discerning about *everything* in our homes. If you don't feel you are able to do that, ask your pastor or one of the church intercessors or a friend with a prophetic gift to walk through your home once.

The Lovely Dolls

God has blessed us with two great "kids." Our son is Matt and our daughter is Angie. Angie used to have a little wooden bench by her doorway where all of her dolls were set up on display. They were just lovely dolls that had been collected from a variety of different sources. Some were expensive and some not. Many were from second hand shops where the original source was not known. As Angie's spiritual eyes began to open more and more, she could not only see angels sometimes but she could also see evil spirits as well. Unfortunately, her dolls had several evil spirits that somehow had managed to hang on and stay there even within the midst of all the prayer etc., that goes on in our home.

Angie's eyes were opened one night and she saw a number of evil spirits coming out of the dolls and into her room. Needless to say, the dolls no longer were welcome. Many would say, why not just pray over the dolls? Well.... If the dolls were that important, I might have prayed over them. But I could not see taking a chance with my daughter's peace and well- being over some dolls. And frankly, they no longer had the same effect on the room after Angie had seen that. She had no desire to keep them.

Angie also then prayed through her closet and pitched many expensive clothes that she felt the Lord say should not be there.

Cleaning the Closet

Matt also had a similar experience one night as he was taken into the spirit and shown a host evil spirits that somehow had gained entrance and were in his closet. He then opened the door and commanded them to leave in Jesus' name. And then he watched them as they obediently marched out .

There is seemingly no end to the different items that can have ties that are unclean. That is why the Holy Spirit should be your guide in these things. Don't be in fear, just continually ask the Lord to expose any darkness and then drive it out of your life.

Go through your stuff and find the things that don't seem to belong. You may have not watched that movie that has been in your TV cabinet for the past twenty years but it can still hold spiritual sway in your home just because it's there. Go through your old CDs and movies. Go through and get rid of anything that ties you to an ungodly relationship.

What is sitting in your house right now that is questionable? What are some areas you could go through just to make sure? Make a list and then pray about those things.

1. _____

2. _____

3. _____

4. _____

5. _____

6. _____

7. _____

8. _____

9. _____

10. _____

Breaking ties to ungodly things

When I find something in my house that I believe may be tainted by the enemy or have some demonic right tied to it, I break any tie off of me and my family / household by the power of Jesus' name.

Let's say for instance it was by a bad choice on my part. A **DVD** for instance. I bought it because it didn't look *that* bad, but having looked at it, they snuck in cursing several times and a mild unclean scene that really doesn't seem *that* bad, but is enough that I have thought about it a few times when I went to my prayer time. So I'm going to throw it away and break off anything demonic that came with it.

Father, In Jesus' name I come to you and I ask your forgiveness for having brought that movie into my home and into my life. I repent and I have thrown it away. In Jesus' name I place this entire scenario under the blood of Jesus. I break any and all ties and soul ties to this object in Jesus' name. I break any and all ties off of me and my family and my home.

I now bind any and all evil spirits connected to this movie from staying here.

I bind you and I cancel your right to be here from my position of authority at the right hand of God and I command you to leave in Jesus' name. I place the blood of Jesus over all images from this movie and I decree that I am cleansed from all unrighteousness in Jesus' name.

If for some reason I still have the occasional foul image pop into my head, I will repeat this process.

A Random Object

Aunt So and so gave us a beautiful silver bracelet before she passed on. It is ornate and expensive and has some intricate writings that we are not sure what they are but every time my wife wears the bracelet she has weird things happen or bad dreams. We have decided to get rid of it. Because of the strange writings on it, I don't want to take the chance and sell it and hand these problems to someone else. So we are throwing it away.

Father in Heaven I plead the blood of Jesus over that bracelet from Aunt So and so and I place the blood of Jesus over my family and home and especially over any and all who have worn that bracelet or come in contact with it. I break any and all power of the enemy off of our lives and our home that are or were connected to the bracelet by the power of the blood of Jesus and the power of Jesus' name. I break every legal right and every tie and soul tie that was upon the bracelet from us in Jesus name and I command all and all evil spirits connected to it in any way to leave now in Jesus' name. Father I thank you for your power to deliver and set free and I thank you for this complete freedom in Jesus name, amen.

Our Children

If we follow the Lord, it makes it so much easier for our kids to follow the Lord also. I know there are situations that can come about as the kids get older, but the Lord has given us promises to hold onto concerning our children.

Train up a child in the way he should go: and when he is old, he will not depart from it. (Proverbs 22:6)

As much as it can look that this verse has no bearing on our reality, this verse *is* our reality. The Word of God is ever more powerful than any circumstance we face and we always have to remember that. Just like anyone else, our children want to belong, to feel like they matter, to feel like they are important. And just like anyone else if they don't get that sense in one way, they will get it from another. There are several evil spirits that try to exert their influence on young people and I will give some examples.

Rebellion and Rejection

These are two spirits that seem to almost always be found working together, especially in young people. The way they "play" it is that a spirit will cause a child to rebel in some way....*"No I won't come home by twelve and you can't make me."* Or *"All the girls dress this way and I'm not going to be the only one who doesn't."* Anyone who has raised or is raising children has their own examples of this. As we deal with these scenarios, it is important that we always remember *who we really are* and operate from a *supernatural perspective.* Our natural reasoning can't always find an answer because there doesn't seem to be any reasoning in the situation. Of course we have to do our best *in love* to set boundaries and consequences, but that in itself is not the extent of what the kids are dealing with. We have to deal with the larger issues connected.

In general because of the stress and sometimes open defiance that can provoke emotional responses, we allow ourselves to be used by a spirit of rejection against the child. The child rebels, we reject the child, the child feels the rejection and rebels even more so we reject the child even more. *"I won't talk to her until she comes and apologizes for everything because she is the one who is in the wrong here!"* Many times the rejection spirit will work in conjunction with a religious spirit. *"You've embarrassed me in front of my church friends for the last time!"* Or *"You are not living up to my spiritual standards so I must reject you."* These are our kids. The level of our responsibility and our authority to help them through these issues is enormous.

When I said that we must deal with issues like this from a *supernatural perspective,* I was not joking. We have incredible power through Christ.

Another example from my own family

I don't want to throw others under the bus unless I have to, but I have plenty of examples from my own life. We are a work in progress.

My wife and my daughter Angie went through a period of time where they were not getting along very well. My wife would ask Angie to go places shopping with her and Angie would go, but after an hour she wanted to be done and she would get "moody" then my wife who wanted Angie to stay with her would get upset because she would look at all the things she did for Angie and she would feel she was due consideration in return. Sometimes occasions like this would blow over and other times it would turn into a week long war of silence. *"No, nothing is wrong. I just don't feel like talking to you."* My wife called me one afternoon from the department store to let me know that it had just gotten bad between her and Angie. They were coming back to the house.

I had been praying for other things when she called, but something rose up in me that said enough is enough. I began binding the work of the enemy in their lives. I bound the enemy over this situation and over their afternoon together. I began to decree that we are God's own family and we do not have to put up with this, and we won't put up with this. I spent the next *two hours* pacing the basement floor decreeing the power and peace of God over my wife and daughter and warring on their behalf. About four hours later they came through the door laughing and smiling and they told me that they just suddenly started getting along better and then had a wonderful afternoon together. The world might say "coincidence", but to the believer who experiences things like this over and over in their lives, we know the truth.

If you can name the thing that is manifesting in your family or in someone's life, you can bind it, defeat it and cast it out. Like rebellion and rejection, we can come against anything and everything not of God and **change the situation**!

Address situations like this every day until there is complete victory. Do not stop! Do it in your own words or exactly like me if you want. Know that you have a legal right by the Word to speak these changes to come to pass and keep at it.

In Jesus' name I bind the spirit of rebellion in _____. I bind you in every way by the power of the blood and name of Jesus Christ and on the authority of the Word. I bind all manifestation, transference and communication in Jesus' name I bind every spirit and evil being working with or giving power to these spirits in Jesus' name. I command you to loose my child. I decree that you are a defeated foe and you have no legal right to stay and afflict them. From God's own right hand I command you to loose them and go. I loose the resources of Heaven against you. I decree that there will be nothing of your evil work left standing. I claim and decree over _____ the complete redemption and restoration power of the blood of Jesus and the manifest power of the Holy Spirit in their life.

Inferiority and insecurity

These are also two spirits who work together in young people to ruin their lives. Inferiority speaks to our children to cause them to feel like they don't measure up or don't really fit in. How does this even get started? Openings that evil spirits will manipulate or take advantage of is a vast area. If one of the parents suffer from this, it can also come upon the children. If a child is not being given a strong sense of who they are at home, in Christ, it leaves them more vulnerable for others to provide that to them. A child taunted at school by one person will often be taunted by many. Then depression and sadness or melancholy will often begin to torment the child as well.

When someone feels inferior their security starts to erode as well. Everything can be called into question whether it is conscious or not. Does anyone still love me. Does anyone really love me if I am not as good as the others? Are my parents just putting up with me or do they care about me? Many relationships that are abusive are fostered by the fact that someone believes that they do not deserve any better.

If we are in a position to speak into someone's life that is battling this, we can use the truth to break off the lie and set them free. The power of the word of God spoken over someone's life can cause these things to fall away, to be destroyed so that they can then receive the truth.

In Jesus' name I bind the spirit <u>inferiority / insecurity.</u> I bind all manifestation, communication and transference of any kind. I bind all related spirits and your work. I decree and command that all of your work and influence is destroyed. I take authority over you by the authority of the Word. I command you to go in Jesus' name. You are a defeated foe. The Lord Jesus spoiled principalities and powers and openly made a show of you. You must go in Jesus' name.

I decree the blessings of God upon _____. I loose perfect love and the knowledge of who _____ is in Christ upon them. I speak and declare boldness in the Holy Ghost upon _____. I decree the righteousness of Christ covers them.

Diagnosing the problem

Any time you are praying for anyone who has or may have spiritual problems or affliction by evil spirits, the Holy Spirit is your best source for knowing what to pray or war about. However, even if you don't have a word of knowledge concerning how to pray, you can usually tell anyway by diagnosing the person's personality. If you make a list of every negative personality "trait", you will probably hit the nail on the head with at least one of those areas.

For instance, if you have a friend who has problems and prayer has not seemed to help them, you could make the list. He seems 1. Angry 2. Bitter 3. Resentful 4. Jealous 5. Unkind 6. Mean and 7. He curses.

As you look over this list, you can see that all of his personality traits seem to have a common theme. There are probably bigger issues than these behind them but as you come against the things you know, the Lord can reveal more and you can address them also.

I would go through the list on behalf of my friend and pray / war in this manner.

In Jesus' name I bind the spirit of anger in _____. I bind all of your manifestation, communication and transference. I command that all of your evil work is destroyed in Jesus name. The Word says that "these signs shall follow those who believe, In my name they shall cast out devils." I am a believer and I now exercise my authority over you and cast you out. Loose _____ in Jesus' name and go.

This is something you can do directly over someone who is willing to receive prayer or someone who is unwilling and is not even in your presence. You are not trying to subjugate their will in any way, but rather to loose their will from any and all evil influences. Although there are exceptions, most people don't want to be miserable and once they have a measure of freedom they can wholeheartedly receive and embrace it.

Is there anyone in your life that you feel could be afflicted in this way? For the sake of discretion, you don't have to write their name but write down or diagnose what their "issues" might be. Pick someone you will want to pray for.

1. _____

2. _____

3. _____

4. _____

5. _____

6. _____

7. _____

8. _____

9. _____

10. _____

I mentioned that our warfare can bring instant release or freedom and sometimes you may pray every day for someone and feel you are getting nowhere. This is where it is important to know that we walk by faith and not by sight. (2 Corinthians 5:7)

Demonic Confrontation

I had been praying every day for someone who I knew needed deliverance. I would spend an hour or so in prayer and warfare, seeing no results of any kind. After about two weeks of this, during a time of intercession, I was sitting on my bed when suddenly two evil spirits materialized in the corner of my bedroom and stood there glaring at me. I knew exactly who they were and it was plain to see that they were angry with my daily binding them in Jesus' name and commanding their work destroyed. I continued without missing a beat and after about twenty minutes they vanished.

If I had been walking by sight, I may never have continued praying due to the fact that it looked as if things were not changing. Things change in the spiritual realm *every time* we pray. We have assurance from the Lord so we continue until the victory is won.

I will also restate that if you are walking in a strong anointing or the Glory of God, the results are very often instantaneous whether the person is with you or not. There is no distance in the spirit realm. That is definitely the place where you want to be!

Who is Qualified?

Age

In my opinion, every person who is born again is qualified (and obligated) to do spiritual warfare. On the basis of Matthew chapter ten we have things that are supposed to follow believers. I think we are obligated to do them by scripture. I have seen kids as young as ten routinely casting out devils and have heard testimonies of parents who have taught their young five or six year olds that if anything "bad" comes into their room to try to scare them, that they should tell it to *"go away in Jesus' name"*. Once the kids see that Jesus has greater power, it becomes very natural to them. Kids seem to "get it" quicker than adults do.

The thing to remember here is that evil spirits have no qualms about attacking children. We have to let the children know that they can tell these "bad" things to go away and they have to obey.

A couple of simple phrases spoken with the faith of a child are all it takes.

Go away in Jesus' name. or **Get out in Jesus' name.**

Personal Walk with God

What about other things that might disqualify a believer from doing warfare, especially in a corporate setting such as a church or ministry? Sin for example? Where do you draw a line when allowing people to minister to others?

I believe that God gives us on the job training in every task He has given us to do. I have never subscribed to the whole "clean yourself up and come to Jesus" and then He will use you mentality.

That being said, it is pointless to have someone living in unrepentant sin "trying" to do spiritual warfare. In the spirit realm, spirits can see who we are and whether we are being real or not. People can fool other people but in the spirit realm things are laid bare. So I would not allow that person to pray for others. It would probably do more harm than good. I would however allow that person to be prayed *for*. They need it.

As far as people wrestling with sins in their life, God will use them. As they pray for others it will hasten their own freedom. I know this from personal revelation and experience.

It was many years ago and I had not yet been delivered from smoking. I knew it was bad for me. It made me feel bad, I didn't sleep so good, I would wake up coughing etc.. So yes, I knew it wasn't something that pleased God. However, I was *willing* to be set free. I had tried to quit at least a hundred times. I prayed about it. I was frustrated by it. I was sick of it. I was sick of trying to quit.

In the midst of this, the Lord put me in a position one day where he used me to bring a young man deliverance from an evil spirit. It was in a church we were visiting one Sunday and at first I didn't react because I didn't feel worthy to help the boy. But the Lord told me I was it. So I did it. That showed me that God will use people in process. (which is most of us)

In Matthew ten it lays out a list of things that Believers are supposed to do. Are there other requirements to be met however and what are they?

Heal the sick, cleanse the lepers, raise the dead, cast out devils: freely ye have received, freely give. (Matthew 10:8)

_____
_____
_____
_____
_____
_____

Knowledge

The Bible says that we shouldn't be ignorant.

Lest Satan should get an advantage of us: for we are not ignorant of his devices. (2 Corinthians 2:11)

If we are to grow, we have to get in the Word of God and study (2 Timothy 2:15) and take advantage of the wisdom and instruction from the Lord conveyed by those who have gone before us. Also, There are anointed people on the Earth today that clearly hear God's voice and have been given wisdom on this topic they share with others. Learn as much as you can. Generally we learn more when we need to learn more. But regardless, I once heard a very successful deliverance minister say, *"If you forget everything you have learned, just remember "Come out in Jesus' name" and you'll be ok."*

Read through the scriptures specifically relating to warfare and study and meditate on them. Revelation is a continuous unfolding. What more can you see? What more has the Lord shown you?

Ephesians 6:10-20 / 2 Corinthians 10:4,5 / James 4:7 / John 10:10 1 Peter 5:8,9 / Romans 8:37-39 / 1 Corinthians 16:13 / Luke 10:19

_____

_____

_____

_____

_____

_____

_____

_____

_____

_____

_____

_____

_____

_____

_____

_____

_____

What can you glean from these scriptures that will help you in warfare? In life?

Dealing with Witchcraft

Charismatic Witchcraft

If you are a believer who believes in and walks in the supernatural power of God, there is a good chance you will deal with this subject. First of all it is sad to say but many times the "witchcraft" we war against is what I call charismatic witchcraft. Curses spoken against us from "well meaning" believers who feel we are off track for what we believe, or perhaps they are angry and convicted and want to be a little vindictive against us so they pray ungodly prayers that actually act as curses, invoking evil spirits.

You know..."*Let them be miserable until they repent!*" or "*I pray their lives will fall apart or sickness come upon them so they see the light!*"

As farfetched as this might seem, I have actually heard prayers like this many times, and have rebuked people for praying them. Unfortunately, I have yet to convince any of them that it is wrong and demonic to pray these types of prayers over people. But because I know I have these types of people in my life, I make sure to deal with it.

When I pray over myself and my family every day, I always address these things.

In Jesus' name, I break the power of the spoken word against me and my family and our household. I break any and all ungodly prayers and Christian curses spoken against us. I command all evil spirits sent by such things to go back where you came from. You are not welcome here.

Witchcraft

As someone who walks in the power and presence of God, you stand out like a beacon in the spirit realm. Many people shine with such a bright intensity in the spirit that others who can see in the spiritual realm can hardly bare to look at them. Any person who operates in any semblance of demonic power can drive by your house and know that a true believer lives there. It is that obvious. Therefore, it is imperative that you plead the blood of Jesus over your family and everything you are and have every day. Break any curses spoken against you and release the Glory of God to surround you like a force field or bubble. Many people in witchcraft are just people who know the supernatural is real and are drawn to it. For so long the church has not presented a true representation but rather "denied the power thereof" so many went into the new age or witchcraft or worse.

I have met witches and new age practitioners who were nice people but deceived in that they don't have the full picture concerning what they are dealing with. I try to look at these people as if they are a loved one who just doesn't yet know how real God is. I don't hate these people and I am not fearful of them. They need to see the light. If I can only be a vessel to give them a taste, many times that's all it takes.

There are also people I have met who are what I would consider "hardcore" witches that have a bone to pick with us and it doesn't matter how kind and loving you are to them, they will try to do you harm. They can't help themselves for that is what is in them. We really have to walk in the spirit and be aware and vigilant concerning this. They do have real power. That is not even a question. But...we have the greater authority. We war or address spiritual problems from our place in Christ. There is nothing to fear.

Behold, I give unto you power to tread on serpents and scorpions, and over all the power of the enemy: and nothing shall by any means hurt you. (Luke 10:19)

If you minister or bring healing or deliverance you can also face opposition. I have been deceived in the past by witches pretending to people who wanted deliverance who come forward just so they can take up the ministry time so that people who really want and need help won't get it. I have also been in Christian homes where the Lord has let me see the opposition and it would seem staggering to see so many evil spirits standing ready to harm someone, but like Elisha prayed for Gehazi....

And when the servant of the man of God was risen early, and gone forth, behold, an host compassed the city both with horses and chariots. And his servant said unto him, Alas, my master! how shall we do? And he answered, Fear not: for they that be with us are more than they that be with them. And Elisha prayed, and said, LORD, I pray thee, open his eyes, that he may see. And the LORD opened the eyes of the young man; and he saw: and, behold, the mountain was full of horses and chariots of fire round about Elisha. (2 Kings 6:15-17)

There was a force field around that kept them at bay. The angels around our lives really do have it covered. The Lord has made sure to protect His own.

There is no end to the stuff they will do though so we have to deal with it. I do it every day as a matter of course. Put on my pants, plead the blood. Put on my shoes, break witchcraft curses. It is a part of being a soldier who is engaged. It is natural and normal.

Being aware is important. Can you think of anything around your life that may smack of witchcraft?

_____

_____

_____

_____

_____

_____

I plead the blood of Jesus over myself and my family. I plead the blood over our home, our work, our health, our finances, our relationships, our generations, our bodies, souls and spirits. I break every hex, vex, jinx, curse, spell, incantation, ungodly prayer or ritual said or done against us in Jesus' name. I break every power of witchcraft, every spoken word, every evil plan by the power of Jesus' name. I break all black magic, voodoo, all bewitchments and enchantments in Jesus name. I call to bear the full weight and measure of the blood covenant of Jesus Christ against the enemy and the resurrection power of the Holy Ghost. I command any and all evil spirits sent to leave in Jesus' name.

Really Mike, aren't you being a little over the top with this?

No.

I have heard testimonies and I have also dealt with these kinds of things and better safe than sorry is my belief. We have been given the power of speaking something so that it might come to pass and I take advantage of that because I know the reality of the warfare.

6

BECOMING NATURALLY SUPERNATURAL

One of the biggest problem with people engaging in spiritual warfare or even healing the sick or doing other supernatural things is that we have not fully embraced our situation. Our reality is that *we are supernatural beings*, born from above, seated at God's right hand, surrounded by a cloud of witnesses and continuously watched over by and ministered to by angels. Supernatural Christianity is not a "fringe" group of believers, it is Christianity itself. You cannot describe Christianity or a relationship with Christ without alluding to the supernatural. Everything about our entire Christian history is supernatural, but we are not living it that way. It makes it hard for the supernatural to feel natural to us if we are not continuously engaging the spiritual realm and reality.

I believe that as the world gets darker, we have to walk in a much greater awareness of who we are and what (who) we carry. We are meant to be the ones who point the way. We are the ones who have supernatural peace in the midst of the storm. We have to train ourselves, our families, our children and our churches to walk in the power of God like it's natural...because it is.

Just like a soldier who is learning to handle a sword, it may feel awkward at first , maybe a little heavy. But as you adjust, it becomes as natural as if it were a part of you.

Accept that God is the Boss

I know it seems funny to say that, but it is true. We have to get over the fact that God may do something outside our comfort zone. If you ask God to increase you or use you let Him decide how, and then go with that.

I will use myself as an example and then a couple of others.

I was seeing very clearly in the spiritual realm for probably a year or more. I saw beings, angels, numbers, objects, demons and a bunch of stuff that I had no understanding for. At one point I began to get anxious. I said *"Lord, if you aren't going to give me understanding, I might as well not see at all."* Big mistake. My ingratitude cut my vision exponentially immediately. I went from seeing all the time to what seemed like merciful sovereign occasions where I could see. Let God be boss and let Him lead the way. We don't need to tell Him what to do or instruct Him in any way.

It wasn't long after God began to do some awesome stuff with our family, visitations, visions etc., when I noticed a disturbing trend among Charismatic ministers at places we went to. I began to notice that from the pulpit, ministers were being dismissive of signs and wonders, being slain in the spirit and other things. I talked to the Lord about this and this is what I felt He impressed upon me. If it is important enough for the Holy Spirit to do it, then honor it. Don't speak against it.

Within a two week period I heard one man say that *"we don't need the gold dust and the other things like that, we need to get back to the "normal" five- fold ministry."* Then, a week later another famous evangelist said *"We don't need all that shaking and stuff like that."* Friends, to me that is dangerous ground. If God does something we need to trust that He knows what He is doing! Let Him be boss and embrace everything He wants to do. If He wants to heal through you, great! If He wants to drop gemstones on your head, Great too! Keep your focus on Christ and be led of the Holy Spirit. Don't make your own limits! It seems that many people believe God is supernatural until He does the supernatural, then they back away. Let the Holy Spirit lead you.

To walk in a place where your warfare is natural and effective, I believe you should continually be engaged with or in the spiritual realm. Learn to walk in both realms and not just mainly in the natural realm except for the times you need to engage Heaven. Be ready at all times because you are already there.

Preach the word; be instant in season, out of season; reprove, rebuke, exhort with all longsuffering and doctrine. (2 Timothy 4:2)

Seven Things You Can Do

1. Prayer

Pray without ceasing. (1 Thessalonians 5:17)

Likewise the Spirit also helpeth our infirmities: for we know not what we should pray for as we ought: but the Spirit itself maketh intercession for us with groanings which cannot be uttered. (Romans 8:26)

Pray in every opportunity that you have. Take stock of your time and see where you can carve out time for prayer. How about while driving to or from work? Going to the store or any long car ride. Or even while drifting off to sleep. When you are not actually praying, keep your heart focused on God still. An attitude of prayer.

I thank my God, I speak with tongues more than ye all: (1 Corinthians 14:18)

Praying in tongues is a way to build up your spirit man. It may feel a little strange to pray for an extended time in tongues, but it brings the supernatural power of God to bear upon you. I pray in tongues as much as I can and you should too.

What are some times and ways that you can make the scripture "Pray without ceasing" a reality?

1. _____

2. _____

3. _____

4. _____

5. _____

6. _____

7. _____

2. Worship Continually

Keep your heart and attitude as one of thankfulness. Sing songs of praise, lift your hands in worship. (I once told the Lord that I wanted to be like those men whom I admired so much and an angel came and let me know it was through worship that this is accomplished.)

Let everything that has breath praise the Lord. Praise the Lord. (Psalm 150:6)

O give thanks unto the LORD; call upon his name: make known his deeds among the people. (Psalms 105:1)

Let the high praises of God be in their mouth, and a two-edged sword in their hand;(Psalms 149:6)

I take many opportunities during my day to worship, even if it's just for five minutes. When can you worship the Lord? When are you most likely to be able to carve out the time?

1. _____

2. _____

3. _____

4. _____

5. _____

6. _____

7. _____

I cried out to him with my mouth; his praise was on my tongue. (Psalms 66:17)

3. Minister Healing and Deliverance Every Day

This is especially important if you are training up your family to walk in the power of God, or training anyone for that matter. To make moving in the gifts *normal*, you should do it as much as possible. Start your day by laying hands on your family and then let them lay hands on you. You say you feel ok....Let them practice on you anyway!

Get your family used to saying the words, invoking the name of Jesus and engaging the spiritual realm. Whether in the morning or at night after everyone is home, take a few minutes and pray a deliverance prayer and a healing prayer over everyone every day and let each person take a turn. Either use these prayers , or make up your own.

Healing

Father in Jesus' name I plead the blood of Jesus over _____. Right now I take authority over all sickness, disease and infirmity and command you to go. I speak complete healing and restoration to _____'s body, soul and spirit. From the top of their head to the souls of their feet I declare complete healing in Jesus' name.

Deliverance

In Jesus' name I take authority over all the power of the devil. I bind everything not of God in _____'s life right now in Jesus' name. I bind everything that would defile or influence _____ in a negative way in Jesus' name and everything that offends the Lord also. I command every negative thing to go in Jesus' name. I decree and declare complete freedom in the Holy Ghost.

These are short and simple prayers and if you make your own, they should be short and simple too. Make it easy for yourself and your family to do this and it will become first nature to you.

Healing

_____

_____

_____

_____

_____

_____

Deliverance

4. Release the Anointing

I learned this at a conference that I went to and to me it made a lot of sense. Don't wait until you are up against it to learn how to release the anointing. Do it every day and learn to move naturally and seamlessly in the anointing and the power of God. How?

You can lay your hand on whatever you want to release the anointing on or into, and decree " I release the anointing in Jesus' name." As you do this, picture or sense or be still enough that you can feel the virtue leaving you as you release it.

When I do this, I like to picture the anointing as a sphere of power about the size of a cantaloupe resting in my hand. I see it, sense it and feel it's weight, then I release it into whatever or whoever I am ministering to. I practice releasing the anointing in my work area, buildings I enter, elevators, door handles, chairs or just anything I feel led to. The reason I picture the anointing as a sphere of power is because I saw it like that once in the spirit and it is something I can lay hold of.

Make your own determination of how you want to do this. Does the anointing you release have color? Substance? Heat? According to your faith be it unto you.

5 . Release the Government of the Kingdom

As an ambassador of Christ, one seated in authority you can call upon the power of God concerning everywhere you set your foot.

Every place that the sole of your foot shall tread upon, that have I given unto you, as I said unto Moses. (Joshua 1:3)

Every place whereon the soles of your feet shall tread shall be yours: from the wilderness and Lebanon, from the river, the river Euphrates, even unto the uttermost sea shall your coast be. (Deuteronomy 11:24)

I release the Government of the Kingdom pretty much everywhere I go and to every building I enter. I would do something like this. I would place my hand on the door jamb or door post and say...

"In the name of Jesus, I release the government of the Kingdom of Heaven over this place."

Sometimes I elaborate...

"I also release the angelic canopy over this place. Let the power of God come upon this place for the glory of the Lord."

If you do this continually, you will make waves in the spirit realm. There is no telling the reaction you will get when you go places throughout your day and release the power of Heaven like this. Once, I went to a medical school to deliver something and when I went to the door a large demonic looking rat about the size of a cat ran through the glass door, out of the building and into the bushes. (The door was closed by the way)

There have been other similar occurrences involving both people and the demonic but that just shows you that you are being effective.

---

6. Practice Hearing God's voice

This is something I learned at another conference and the Lord confirmed the validity of it using my own daughter. At a conference my son Matt and I went to in Moravian Falls, North Carolina, we were asked to do an exercise where we close our eyes, picture a scene from the Bible and place ourselves within the scene. Then we were to ask the Lord a question and listen to His response.

Matt did this exercise and the Lord told him something that ministered to him. When I did this exercise, when I asked the Lord what He wanted to tell me, He said *"Mike I have great plans for you but you need to be obedient."* That sounded accurate to me. When we got home from the conference I was telling my daughter Angie about the exercise and asked her to give it a try. She said *"I don't know what I should ask. "*I told her to just ask the Lord if He had a word for me then. She said *""Ok."*

So Angie closed her eyes and was still for a couple of minutes. *"I don't know about this Dad."* I said *"What? Just tell me."* She said *"Jesus said you need to obey ."*

It is an easy way to learn to hear God's voice. Within a few minutes a day, you can learn to hear God's voice and as you engage everyday it becomes clearer and clear.

_____
_____
_____
_____
_____
_____
_____

7. Words of Knowledge

This is a fun and easy way to learn how to move in words of knowledge. Using whatever method you are most comfortable with, ask the Lord for words of knowledge for people that you might see throughout the day, for healing or encouragement or anything really.

I would use a notebook to write everything down because it is a proof that God told you beforehand what you are sharing rather than you saying God told you to speak to a forty year old woman with red hair and a green hat carrying a leopard print purse. If you have it written down it will carry more weight.

Write down as many descriptions of people as you feel the Lord is giving you. Then, whatever specific words of knowledge the Lord is giving you for them. (Healing, etc..)

The great thing about this exercise in delivering words of knowledge is that there is no pressure as you get comfortable with this. The weight is entirely on the Lord. If you write down ...middle aged man with white hair, jeans and a mickey mouse sweatshirt walking with a cane and a limp who needs a supernatural knee replacement, and you don't see him, no problem.

But if you do see him, you know definitely it is a word from God. You show him how specific God spoke to you about him by showing him your book, and it will open a door for you to pray for him.

You may think that you would never hit the nail on the head but the very first time Matt and I did this when we went out for coffee one day, we found the person within fifteen minutes and the word about back pain was accurate and even verified by the girl's friend. God will train you and make it easy for you to learn to be naturally supernatural.

_____
_____
_____
_____
_____
_____
_____
_____

An Explanation of This Chapter

All of these little morsels of engaging with the spirit realm are meant to keep you engaged on an ongoing, everyday basis. The fact that all of these exercises can be done at different points in your day or throughout your day, is purposeful so that you are constantly walking in the natural and spiritual realms all through the day.

If you desire to walk in both realms you have to walk in both realms! At first, many of the things presented you will be engaging by faith, but soon enough the Lord will confirm that you are connecting with Heaven and that will encourage you even more.

Michael Van Vlymen

About the Author

Michael Van Vlymen is a writer and speaker who has a passion to share with people the reality of the supernatural things of God. Along with his wife Gordana Van Vlymen, they founded River of Blessings International Ministries to facilitate the teaching of these types of subjects for end times ministry for the body of Christ.

www.riverofblessingsinternationalministries.org

Also by Michael Van Vlymen

How to See in the Spirit – A Practical Guide On Engaging The Spirit Realm
* Available in several languages

Angelic Visitations and Supernatural Encounters – A Diary of Living in the Supernatural of God

21757784R00058

Printed in Great Britain
by Amazon